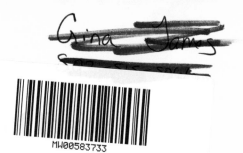

Wor

I found *Images of Soul* to be a creative, original, and inspiring example for clinicians like myself who see it as part of our life's work to merge the astrological and psychological perspectives in a clinical setting. The images of soul explored throughout this book forge a creative pathway toward the deeper fusion of psychotherapy and astrology—the two companionable modes of perceiving psyche.

> -- Gisele Terry, MFT, President, International Society for Astrological Research

An occasion for the reader to dip a toe into the sacred pond of Imagination, *Images of Soul* is an intimate conversational portrait disclosing the living waters of Psyche. It revivifies and deepens the trivialized remains of a once vibrant and animated wisdom tradition, bringing it new life.

> -- Brad Kochunas, author of *The Astrological Imagination*

Judith and Hadley have created something very special and unique in exploring the resonant space between depth psychotherapy and astrology. I love the book!

-- Brockton Hill, JD, MFT, Jungian Analyst/Archetypal Astrologer

IMAGES OF SOUL
REIMAGINING ASTROLOGY

Hadley Fitzgerald, M.A.
Judith Harte, Ph.D.

Iris & Acorn Press

Images of Soul
Reimagining Astrology

ISBN-13: 978-0692270530
ISBN: 0692270531

Printed in the United States of America

Iris & Acorn Press
For information contact:
IrisandAcornPress@gmail.com

Cover Design by Jill Bell
Acorn Image Created by Matthew Jones

Table of Contents

Dedication

To the enigmatic call of our daimons, those prime movers of
psyche's soulful maps,
whether in life after life or one life at a time.

Epigraph

To exist as an individual is to undergo a process of actualization of what, at birth, was mere potentiality. Your chart is the acorn of the oak you can become, within the limits imposed by the conditions prevailing in the biosphere and in your society at that time and during your lifetime. It informs you of the manner in which you can best answer the need of the universe at the time and place you became linked to it—associated with it—by your first breath, your first response to an open environment. (The mother's womb is a closed environment; you can only struggle against it.) But once the rhythm of your breathing and the complete circulation of the blood—through the lungs as well as through the whole body—is set, you have become an actor on the world stage. You have a role to play in the universe.
-- Dane Rudhyar In "The Birth Chart as a Celestial Message" AFA talk in 1976

The acorn theory proposes and I will bring evidence for the claim that you and I and every single person is born with a defining image. Individuality resides in a formal cause—to use old philosophical language going back to Aristotle. We each embody our own idea, in the language of Plato and Plotinus. And this form, this idea, this image does not tolerate too much straying. The theory also attributes to this innate image an angelic or daimonic intention, as if it were a spark of consciousness; and, moreover, holds that it has our interest at heart because it chose us for its reasons.
-- James Hillman, *The Soul's Code: In Search of Character and Calling*, pp. 11-12

Life is a luminous pause between two mysteries that yet are one.
-- C.G. Jung, 9. 2 or 36.31

Appreciation

To C.G. Jung for everything

To the late James Hillman, an essential figure in our souls' codes. We honor him from the innermost recesses of our literal and imaginal hearts

To Richard Tarnas with profound gratitude for his deeply acute past, present, and no-doubt-future historical, educational, archetypal, and astrological eye

To the late Richard Idemon for his pioneering work in articulating "the divine marriage" between astrology and psychology and for introducing Judie and Hadley to one another

To Steven Forrest who has posited a fully developed, truly soulful model of Evolutionary Astrology

To Barry Miller, clinical psychologist/Jungian analyst, for his early acceptance, understanding, and honoring of what has turned out to be a hearkening of things to come in the field of astrological psychology

To Bonnie Bright for the Depth Psychology Alliance, a courageous online global community that gracefully honors and contains the heart and soul of an Imaginal Astrology

To Pacifica Graduate Institute for its very existence and its magical, mythical sense of place

To the Images for continuing to show up

To our clients who trust us with their souls

To our astrological ancestors who endured all manner of challenges to keep astrology alive, thus passing down to us—and many others—the opportunity to reimagine it for future generations

Regarding the Cover Art

An acorn, alchemical colors, horoscopes as astrological timepieces

It started with the acorn. Throughout this book we refer to the "acorn theory" James Hillman puts forth so beautifully in *The Soul's Code: In Search of Character and Calling*. It's the perfect image to illustrate the soul's metaphorical and mythical movement in and out of time, as shown within the birth horoscope. And thanks to Hadley's late night internet search—which led us to Portland, Oregon photographer Matthew Jones—a perfect 21st century acorn, one that evokes nature, technology, and the mysterious nature of time, found us!

Here we see the acorn's inner mechanism, its movement through time by the clock, by the year, by the century. The oak tree requires some 60 years to mature and produce its first full crop of fruit; the typical development of the tree includes a period of rapid growth for upwards of 80+ years. In that simple, earthy, soulful acorn resting on a round base resembling the astrological wheel, we see the carrier and determiner of the tributaries and permutations of our individual and perhaps even collective fate; and we offer gratitude to it for calling to our attention, in such a wondrous way, to its very particular way of telling time. Now, after a period of thirty-plus years, our own acorn-driven quest has led to the completion of *Images of Soul: Reimagining Astrology*.

Only after we chose the colors for our book's squared-off, no nonsense, and perhaps a bit too academic-looking cover, did we realize that our palette of velvety black, deep and bright reds, gold, and the starry-white womb of the astrological circle, was analogous to the prominent colors in Jung's work on psychological alchemy. While meaningful in themselves, those colors would've been far less so without the presence of this particular acorn containing its very own time piece. To us, it evokes the marking of time we see within nature and in the eternal mystery of our own lives. Throughout this book we ask you to keep in mind that, whether in past, present, or future lives, we are each driven by our acorn's unique inner movement, by an invisible, timeless, yet time-keeping mechanism of destiny and soul.

Hadley Fitzgerald, M.A.
Judith Harte, Ph.D.

Preface

Origin

While reorganizing her tiny home office a while back, Judie found an old rumpled cardboard box and heard herself ask out loud, "What's this?" She lifted the tattered cover and found a long-forgotten, eighty-plus page assemblage of letters and writings coauthored in the late eighties with colleague, friend, and astrologer-psychotherapist, Hadley Fitzgerald. After reading through the first twenty pages, she closed the thick folder and sat in stunned silence. In that moment, quite the way one feels when realizing they've been pierced by the arrow of Eros, she had the feeling of falling in love.

Twenty-seven years earlier Hadley had made a pioneering move east to take a position created specifically for her. She was to explore the ways in which astrology and family systems theory could be integrated for use in an academic residential treatment facility. Just as Hadley was departing, Judie embarked on the writing of her doctoral dissertation. She placed a phone call to noted astrologer, author, historian, and educator Richard Tarnas who was then in residence at Northern California's Esalen Institute. She had an idea related to her dissertation proposal and wanted to run it by him.

He had no idea who she was back then, but he took her call. She'd hoped to add another category of thought to the burgeoning body of psychological astrology and asked for his feedback. This project was to involve integrating and incorporating the work of archetypal psychologist and Jungian analyst James Hillman (now deceased) into the astrological counseling process. It would have the working title: *An Imaginal Approach to Astrological Psychology*. Rick was kind, helpful, and supportive throughout the conversation, and she has never forgotten his specific words just before they rang off:

"If you do this, you will raise the level of astrology."

With no one else to talk to in depth at that time and with a desire to explore this new approach, Judie started writing to Hadley. This not only got some thoughts down on paper, but it also led Hadley to describe what she was experiencing as she focused on applying astrology in a specific clinical setting. Over the course of just a few months they exchanged several letters.

Evolution

The letters we exchanged during that time in our lives serve as impetus for this book. The evolution of that correspondence can be found in Parts One, Two, and Three. When we began to edit the material in those typewritten letters, many questions arose that invited further exploration and discussion. In the intervening years James Hillman's *The Soul's Code: In Search of Character and Calling* had been published to wide acclaim; and it was immediately obvious to both of us what a superb case he'd made for the resonance between the guiding daimon's plan—i.e., the soul's code—and the map of that plan as shown in the astrological chart. As we reflected on where our personal lives and professional practices have taken us, and in the spirit of honoring what's apparently been waiting to be reimagined outside that box Judie found, we decided to correspond again. So we've incorporated what for us has been an exciting, contemporary email exchange. We offer that correspondence in Part Four.

The still-fertile thoughts culled from Judie's doctoral dissertation easily combine with Hadley's experience using astrology as an individual and systemic psychodiagnostic tool and with her ongoing interest in how her astrological clients' evolutionary dilemmas and processes present themselves in the chart. In Part Five we provide a brief clinical case study joining the imaginal and evolutionary perspectives so that readers can have some idea of how we approach this kind of work. In Part Six there is an exploration of comparative astrological perspectives, both in terms of how these have evolved over time as well as how they might also be integrated in one or more consultations.

While somewhat ahead of their time many years ago, we believe the ideas put forth in this book beg for elaboration as to their professional relevance in the here and now. And so we present *Images of Soul: Reimagining Astrology*.

We are aware that there could be times when the reader might feel lost regarding certain terms and definitions. We've done our best to attend to this dilemma, yet there are places where we may have failed in this regard. We refer the reader to the bibliography for further elucidation.

Wherever the precise sources of quotations can be cited, we've done so. However, given that decades have elapsed since our early correspondence, and that at times we cited only the author when exchanging quotations, a few of the quotes we still find so relevant are offered without their specific source. Any clarification readers can provide is most welcome.

All names and identifying characteristics—other than astrological data—have been changed to preserve confidentiality.

Introduction

The vast difference between astrology and other sciences, if I may put it thus, is that astrology deals not with facts but with profundities. The solid ground on which the scientist pretends to rest gives way, in astrology, to imponderables.

-- Henry Miller

Rilke's idea that there is in us all "something helpless that wants help from us"[1] is one to which most workers in the helping professions can surely resonate. Discovering what that "something" is and how to help it is a part of each individual's life journey, and the search often brings a client into the office of both astrologers and psychotherapists.

We are astrological psychotherapists—i.e., licensed practitioners of psychotherapy who use the birth horoscope in order to help access and understand the human psyche. The birth horoscope is here defined as an astronomical map calculated for the precise moment and place of birth and represented on paper by means of a symbolic astrological alphabet.

We take the position that astrology has value as a theory of personality, a counseling tool, and that it also has clinical

---

[1] Rilke, Rainer Maria. *Letters to a Young Poet*, W.W. Norton & Co., New York, 1962, p. 69

implications for psychotherapy. Such an assumption rests, however, upon the documented opinions of only a select body of thinkers. History has given us many contrary assumptions about, and opinions of, astrology; and all of them can be gathered to represent the position that astrology is an unorthodox, heretical agglomeration of hit-and-miss, hocus-pocus beliefs in the midst of which lies very little of value.

Be that as it may, astrology has survived and, in its more traditional aspects, has generally been concerned with using the map of the birth horoscope in order to study, interpret, or "read" individual character traits and/or predict personal life events. Yet in tracing the developments within the astrological field, it is clear that, in its contemporary application, astrology has become increasingly psychological in nature. And when astrological consultations include the guidance of a licensed psychological professional, we believe that the client's experience is greatly enriched. Supported by our many years of experience, we hold the idea that astrology acts as a mirror to the human psyche and that, in so doing, astrology and psyche speak a similar language: that of image.

Imaginal Psychology attempts to "know" the psyche in terms of its images. These images are taken as the primary nature and reality of the psyche's experience. Thus we could say that, in various ways, psyche seeks to express itself and let itself be known through the images it presents to us. This expression is neither linear nor conceptual—it is, rather, an experience.

In approaching psychological astrology from this imaginal perspective, the birth horoscope is seen as a diagram of the interaction of planetary gods, deities, or archetypes who are also sources of these psychic images. As such, *images of the horoscope = images of the psyche, the soul,* and an engagement via verbal or written dialogue, storytelling, dream work, etc., with those images is an invaluable means for bringing psyche more fully into one's life.

Entire books and numerous articles have been written about imaginal psychology, the imaginal perspective in psychotherapy, and the myriad ways in which image can—and must—address the near-catastrophic rift between contemporary thought and a soulful view of the world. At the same time some specific definition of the word "imaginal" and the imaginal realm might be desirable, it also seems frustratingly contradictory. How can we concretize something functioning perfectly but in another realm entirely? The most succinct offering we can make here is to cite David Miller: "This is a realm *between* that of the mind and that of experience, between idea and reality, between ideal and real, between infinite and finite."[2] Or, in an attempt to offer you an image(!) of the imaginal realm: think of it as the sound that exists between the black and white keys. Or, in astronomical terms, the "heliopause" or "wind between the worlds" as Carl Sagan described it.

---

[2] Miller, David L. *Christs: Meditations on Archetypal Images in Christian Theology, Volume 1.* The Seabury Press-New York, 1981, p. xxii

The goal of an imaginal psychological astrology is to attend to the images as given by the birth horoscope. To be image-focused is to have these images as paradigms at the center of a therapeutic process. The Greek noun "therapeia" and verb "therapevo" can be defined as "waiting on, tending to, fostering; nurture, care; to do service to the gods, to attend to, to heal, to cure." [3] Thus psychotherapy is attending to, nurturing the soul—and therefore listening deeply to what it has to say. Tending and attending to these images of soul is precisely that. If, as Jung said, "image is psyche," then "where better to hear what our souls want than in the images that intimately speak to our psychic conditions ?"[4]

As trained and seasoned astrologers, counselors, or licensed psychotherapists, we understand that our first responsibility is to listen to the client and to assess the current level of anxiety, distress, and pain present in the treatment room. As Theodore Roszak noted, "Ultimately, no system is any better than the judgment and honesty of those who use it. Wisdom and decency are qualities of people, not of systems."[5] We concur. Therefore, it is of course vital to have a sound theoretical base and solid training in systemic and personal dynamics when working with people in the complex sphere of psychotherapy, and we are not proposing any substitute for that foundation. Nor are we suggesting that clients with objections to astrology be in any way influenced to embrace

---

[3] Liddell & Scott's *Greek-English Lexicon*, 7th Edition. Oxford: Oxford University Press, 1997, p. 362

[4] Hillman, James. *Healing Fiction*, Stationhill Press, Barrytown, NY, 1983, p. 91

[5] Roszak, Theodore. "Why Astrology Endures: The Science of Superstition and the Superstition of Science," Robert Briggs Associates, San Francisco, CA, First Broadside Edition, 1986.

it. We do propose that one of the methods in which the human psyche may be more *deeply* known, and its particular purpose or intention understood, is by attending to the images that arise within the astrotherapeutic setting. This can be accomplished without resorting to conceptualization, symbolization, or reductive causal diagnostic determinations.

Given a solid professional foundation, we're suggesting when an imaginal approach to psychological astrology is employed, the client is stirred in ways that not only deepen the functioning of his or her psychic processes, but also penetrate and affect multiple dimensions of experience in the everyday world. An imaginal approach asks for a dedication to the images of the horoscope for their own sake. A healing, a "making whole," is possible by tending to the images that psyche, the soul, presents. Hillman postulated that it's the image(s) that wants or needs to be healed—and not just us as source of these images. We cannot know what it is that the astropsychological images want until we have attended to them without imposing upon them a specific agenda. If healing occurs in whatever form, then that's what wants to happen. Even so, this healing is not the sole purpose of giving attention to the images; they are worth waiting upon for themselves.

In our culture images are relentlessly supplied for us. We are inundated, bombarded, swamped by them to the point that we have so focused on what's "out there" we are in peril of losing all connection with the inner life of the soul and its ability to communicate with us through the only means it has: its images. Many years ago Chief Oren Lyons suggested, from the Native American perspective, the droughts befalling us are due to our culture's failure to have reverence for the rain gods. These gods do not feel welcome and their function and presence are devalued, so they withdraw their energy and their gift of rain from us altogether. It seems to the authors we do something similar with images: we fail to give them a place of honor, so they leave us impoverished, our souls dried out. Hence: psychopathology ("psyche-pathos-logos")—literally, the language of the suffering soul.

As indicated in the preface, this book evolved out of a correspondence between two friends who are also astrological and therapeutic colleagues. When Hadley moved to New England in 1987 to become the astrological therapist-in-residence at a private residential facility for adolescents, she was challenged with setting up a treatment program using astrology as a therapeutic tool for dealing with troubled kids and their equally troubled family systems. The letters between the two of us were generated as Judith began seriously to consider how she might honor her own desire to bring an imaginal psychological approach to the understanding of the birth horoscope in a way that would be accessible to astrologers, astrological psychotherapists, and other psychologically oriented professionals who seek to bring other dimensions to their work.

As with most mental health professionals, both of us have experienced "the loneliness of the long-distance therapist" over the years; there are simply not that many people with whom one can talk about what it means to plumb the breadth and depth of the human soul on a daily basis. Factor the language and perspective of the astrologer into that ongoing experience, and the sense of isolation has a near-Promethean quality at times. When Hadley moved east, both of us soon realized how much we had taken for granted the connection and support we so readily gave each other. The geographical separation jarred both our perspectives and, as best we can articulate it, seemed to demand we make room for something new to grow between us. We had never had occasion to write one another at length, but in a short time our letters began to unveil and illuminate the interpersonal and intrapersonal experiences we shared. We remain friends whose lives have continued to expand to accommodate ideas and possibilities that, as of this writing, can't be embraced by the great majority of people around us.

In addition, our correspondence and friendship have bridged the shift from 20th century typewritten letters mailed across the continent to 21st century emails exchanged from a distance of only ten miles. We hope the material generated between us will stimulate readers to engage the images they themselves discover as they explore with us this process of pioneering and applying imaginal psychology to the understanding of the astrological chart. It is our prayer that in so doing we can all offer a lifeline to those vulnerable and neglected images of soul which need only our help to be seen at last as beautiful and brave.

Hadley Fitzgerald, M.A.
Judith Harte, Ph.D.

Elaboration

As a way of introducing the reader to the perspective of imaginal astropsychology, here are the essential parts of a dialogue we got into while working on the introduction to this book. To wit:

HF: Remind me: Where did the term "images of soul" come from?

JH: Years ago I read some place that the images of the psyche are also known as images of soul. The phrase caught me. As you know, I used it in the dissertation; and then I slowly began to use it more and more when analyzing horoscopes. The next step really came about one day quite a while later as I worked on one client's horoscope. A phrase came to me, or perhaps it was a sentence or two, and I soon found myself describing a short vignette in a few lines. It was a kind of word picture or image that described the essence of this chart as I worked on it in that moment. I brought it in and gave it to the client. This was kind of gutsy because I had no guarantee that what I was describing would resonate with the person, or how she would receive it.

HF: Did it give you a deeper insight into the chart? The client?

JH: That one did. Then, if I was working with clients on their progressions or a solar return, I often saw that an image also might be relevant for a particular year, a particular cycle in the life.

What fascinated me then is that I seemed to access a kind of faith during that process. I never worried about whether the client or patient would receive the information positively or disagree with it. I was concerned it might be taken as hocus-pocus or some kind of inflation on my part, but the experience hasn't been like that at all. Then one day something else that I hadn't expected happened on the spot. I suggested the client might engage in an imaginal dialogue with her image of soul.

HF: For example?

JH: The image I gave her was: *An elderly Chinese couple sits quietly at the kitchen table while their extended family serves them dinner. The setting is calm and filled with an elegant simplicity.*

HF: Did that resonate with her? Was she of Asian descent?

JH: When that image first appeared I hadn't met her yet. It turned out she wasn't Asian at all. She was Caucasian, American, single, a retired college professor born at the New Moon in Sagittarius placed at the cusp of the 4th house (home, family, tradition). As I worked on her horoscope before our meeting, this image simply came. Perhaps I was reaching for one version of the ideal manifestation of a Sun/Moon in Sadge in the 4th. But I never try to create an image according to any specifications. It's either there or it isn't, and I receive it as it is. Actually, when this process first occurred I resisted it. The last thing I ever want to be associated with is something reminiscent of fortune telling. You know, like dial-a-psychic for your image of soul!

HF: I know that feeling!—and I had a similar initiating experience with an image in my first year of private practice—I'll tell you later. Was your client moved by this image?

JH: Yes, and I asked her if she would like to have a dialogue with it. At first she was taken aback, so I offered it to her to take home and contemplate. She took it and sent me a note containing some of the dialogue she'd eventually explored. Turns out the image of soul reflected many things in her life that had been missing.

HF: So you'd tuned in on what was absent.

JH: Yes, the image articulated a metaphor, an ideal; and in her case, the living embodiment of pieces or parts of it might still be possible in one form or another. What I articulated to her was basically that the astrological design pointed to a need to incorporate, perhaps expand, something foreign into her home ground.

HF: So, in part, that was a calling in her to bring the faraway Sagittarius into the everyday 4th: actual home? Internal home?

JH: Perhaps both. And the challenges—or ease—of doing that depended on the other planetary configurations within her chart and the stress or ease with which her astrological archetypal complexes engaged or not.

HF: Or if that was her daimon's or guiding angel's agenda for her.

JH: To me a daimon *is* an angel.

HF: Well said.

A cautionary note: The imaginal dialogues described throughout this text are to be engaged in with clients who are already in a process of psychotherapy with a licensed professional or who are clients of an experienced astrologer, someone capable of discerning who may or may not be an appropriate candidate for this work—and who, when imaginal work is attempted and the material emerging in the session becomes clinically complex, knows when to stop and to subsequently refer to a licensed psychological professional.

PART 1

Endearing Distance

Destiny is our mythical sense of life. We get the feeling about our life that something is meant, something is wanted, something is living alongside my life nudging, urging, sometimes grabbing the wheel and setting another course.

-- James Hillman, *The Soul's Code*

August 30, 1987

Dear Hadley,

How does it feel to be anticipating an autumn on the other side of the continent? Are you settled yet? Your courage astounds me. Of course it's too soon to tell whether your excursion to the East Coast will be all that you've imagined it might be, but speaking of imagining, I've enclosed a gift, *The Thought of the Heart*, by Jungian analyst James Hillman. This little gem of a book speaks psychologically of heart, courage, and the will of the lion. He refers to the heart as "the place of true imagining." I thought of you when I read this book— after all, dear friend, it is your heart that led you east, and no doubt you've left behind a piece of your heart here in Southern California.

I have many ideas about "our" work which I am eager to explore and discuss with you in the coming months. What it is. What it isn't. What it might be. I've been contemplating the usefulness of yet another aspect of astropsychological experience which I'm eager to share with you. So get ready for some Lion-talk! I can already sense the impending loneliness out here in the land between astrology and psychotherapy. No colleague waiting nearby, toll-free, to discuss the countless aspects, challenges, and difficulties, clinical as well as personal, which confront that rare breed of cat (or is it lion?), the astrological psychotherapist.

But these can wait until your boxes are unpacked and you are well placed in your new world.

Love, J.

September 6, 1987

Dear Judie,

Thank you for your kind letter and that perfect little gift, *The Thought of the Heart*. You speak of my "excursion" to the East Coast and, since you know my love of words, you'll forgive my immediate referral to the dictionary to see what psyche (yours) intended by selecting that particular one (Russell Lockhart's *Words As Eggs* being my driver here.) I found the first and fifth meanings to be interesting brackets for this experience, to wit: "a short journey or trip to some point for a special purpose, with the intention of a prompt return," and (physics) "the displacement of a body or a point from a mean position of neutral value, as in oscillation." I experience my dear friends as holding the first definition in their minds and hearts, while, at this juncture, the thought of my heart seems to go toward the theme of displacement and oscillation.

This "summons" east was so sudden that I had no time to contemplate the myriad levels on which my heart might be affected. Indeed, the opportunity to do this work we love so much in an environment where thoughts and hearts might truly be engaged and where, therefore, individual and collective lives might be re-imaged (re-imagined?) was utterly compelling. While you see me as embarking on the experience with courage, I wouldn't equate that with "bravery," as I believe you do sometimes.

Rather, I would go to the "coeur" in "courage" as being most apt, because in moments of gravest doubt and fear (there were many such moments—especially as I drove across the country alone) I'd summon the words of Castañeda's don Juan: "For me there is only the traveling on paths that have heart, on any path that may have heart." I taped that sentence to my dashboard when I was getting divorced many years ago, separating from the place where my heart had resided with such certainty for so long. So, here I was—going through another kind of divorce, this one even more wrenching in many ways, and don Juan's words were often like a torch guiding me forward. I had the image of the centaur's flaming arrow being fired into the unknown, yet attached by a heartstring to my Jupiter in Leo-ness/Lioness—I saw that arrow being fired across the country from California to the Atlantic Coast.

My heart was also en-couraged to bring me here by a powerful dream I had exactly one month after dear Richard [Idemon] died in February. I told my therapist about it, but no one else. In the dream I'm sitting in a completely white room—at a white table, on a white chair. Richard walks into the room in his familiar black turtleneck and black slacks. He's radiant, looks so happy and full of life. I'm full of tears—happy to see him yet aware he's died. I say: "Richard, what am I to do now?" He smiles and says, "You're to make a bridge between Anna's generation and what I've taught you." Then he was gone.

I had that dream at my dear friend Ellen's house while I was staying with her not far from where Richard had lived. I couldn't make sense of it at all. Anna is her teenage daughter—but at that time I hadn't been particularly involved in working with teenagers therapeutically or astrologically.

Then a month to the day after that, I had the interview with Adrian in LA. He said those magic words: "I want you to come do astrology and your therapy work and help my kids. I'll do whatever it takes to get them across the bridge back into the world. You design the program, you show us how to do this." As you know (and I know you had your reservations), I agreed on the spot, and things went very quickly from there. But as I drove away from the interview that day I did have misgivings about my haste. Then halfway up Hilgard Ave. the dream about Richard swooped into my mind; I started to shake, had to pull over, stop the car. It was all there: Anna's generation, "bridge," the opportunity to use what Richard taught me. I'm still reeling from his death, but being here keeps some kind of connection.

In any case, you're quite right. A piece of my heart is left behind in California. That I would find it hard, pain-full to go away from friends of so many years was to be expected (at least my intellect could look ahead and anticipate those feelings.) What I could not have imagined were the feelings attendant on separating from clients. We live and work, you and I, in this world which weaves symbols and sympathies in so complex a tapestry that, on the one hand, we are blessed with some sense of the orderliness of "it" all, yet we cannot do the work without our hearts being engaged with each of these human beings. Eros, the life-connecting principle, must somehow be present, or the process won't work. And so I had to weep and grieve the severing of each of those therapeutic relationships, some 20 or so. I carried the image of the lioness leaving her cubs at various ages and stages, and hoping she's imparted some fier(fire)ceness somewhere along the way.

My intense grieving served to remind me that the heart does not engage in this work lightly regardless of what the mind knows. We create an entity, a container, each of these people and I—a sacred place where we go each week and do what we can in the realm of heart and soul to imagine that life might be different somehow. Without that imaging and without the heart that opens to it, the soul (*psyche*) does not heal (*therapevo*.) And so to come to each of these individuals and say that I would not be able to meet them in this place anymore constellated in me something I'm not sure I can describe. The aforementioned image of the fiery arrow yanking my heart by its heartstring is as close as I can come. A very business-oriented client of mine, watching me weep profusely, observed in our last session: "Gee, you don't get to give your notice just once, do you?" I'm also aware that the order of things therapeutic is that the client leaves the therapist, and I'm not sure what psyche makes of what I did.

All of this was transpiring, as you know, with transiting Saturn conjunct my Sun—the Ineluctable conjoining the Developing Self. I suspect that that particular configuration— Time pressing on the Heart?—can only engage the latter in quite a tug-of-war, a pulling forward by what is imagined and a pulling back by what is imagined as well. Some decision of major consequence (Saturn) is made in the space in between. The words to the song from "The Fantasticks" played through my head a lot: "Without a hurt, the heart is hollow." You and I and most of those we know, my friend, are in no danger of having hollowed hearts.

The farewell gathering of wonderful women in my life, however, so filled my heart; and I could've had such a wonderful experience only because I was leaving—no other event would have called forth those particular energies. I felt blessed beyond measure as I embarked on the 3,000-mile drive across the "heartland" of America. A few moments ago, I looked up "heart" in my *Synonym Finder*, and there's a listing of the many expressions in which the word is used:

after one's own heart
at heart
break (someone's) heart
by heart
cross one's heart
do one's heart good
eat one's heart out
from the bottom of one's heart
have a change of heart
to one's heart's content
with one's heart in one's mouth
heartache
heartbreak
heartburn
heartfelt
hearth (Hestia's domain!)
heartsick
heartwarming

I have a feeling (in my heart? where else?) that by the time this experience is whatever constitutes "over," I will have had more than a passing acquaintance with all of the above.

And so, I put this edition—and me—to bed for this night. I welcome this exchange and am eager to see what waits for us in it.

Love,
H.

September 18, 1987

Dear Hadley,

Your wonderful letter filled me with a multitude of images. I couldn't wait to answer it. I read it through and then I performed a private little ritual. In this ritual I willingly surrendered the comfortable closeness of our neighborly friendship to the highly imaginative but terribly inconvenient long distance. Can one willingly surrender? Is that a contradiction in terms or just another word-image for the conjunction of the astrological Pluto (Will) and Neptune (Surrender)?

Our geographical separation has intensified my interest in a mutual exploration of those elusive images of psyche and horoscope in quite a particular way. My psyche's interior landscape is beginning to thrive on the separation.

Last night at 3:00 a.m. I awakened from a dream:

> *You and I sat on top of a hill overlooking a canyon. We were sitting directly on the ground at the entrance to a long cone-shaped cave. The earth was dry, dusty and rocklike, the sun felt bright and hot. We sat side by side. We each had one palm pressed firmly on the ground supporting our bodies. We looked back over our shoulders into the dark cave, trying to see into its depths. (We were posed rather like the woman in that Andrew Wyeth painting.)*

Having each arrived at our professional destinations, is there now a need to look back, to look again, into that dark matrix that contained us in our journey? Did we ever take the journey at all? Or, are we meant to take the journey again, supported by the body's flesh and the "working hands," warmed by the Leonine solar light of consciousness?

I couldn't fall back to sleep. I reflected on a time about ten years ago.

I recalled one day how you as unofficial therapist intervened, oh so skillfully, as we were talking on the phone. You, already a graduate student in psych and family therapy and me, painfully undulating between the nightly practice of underground astrology and the daily routines of office administration in the plastic world of plastic surgery. For the umpteenth time I bemoaned what I assumed was my irrevocable fate. I, too, longed to return to graduate school.

Could it ever happen? You responded to my Moon's Capricornian pessimism. In a simple sentence you reframed and beautifully converted my angst into pure Sagittarian possibility. The sentence went something like this: "Judie, for years I have been hearing you say how much you want to return to school." You then paused long and purposefully. In your words I heard my angst.

Yet, contained within that precise pause were unverbalized possibilities. In that silence I heard you say, "It's O.K. You can do it." Was the psychological mechanism of projection at work here? Of course. I needed to attribute possibility to your unformed words, to hear you tell me what I couldn't tell myself. I needed you to grant me permission to act.

Not long after that conversation I acted. I entered school and reclaimed this brave notion as my own idea. With my psyche wrapped in virginal images of one day practicing astrology and psychotherapy side by side, I followed you into the official world of academia. A world where now years later we each wrestle with our own and our patients' personal, and in Jung's terms, collective/archetypal struggles. In that academic world of tests, grades, case conferences and licenses, one is hard-pressed to gain preparation for the kind of soul-wrenching "good-byes" which you experienced with your patients prior to leaving Southern California. No psychological theory of personality or slick analysis of astrological symbols can prepare one for what happens in the room where psyche meets psyche. Or, as you so eloquently stated, there is no way to forecast outcomes in "that sacred place where we go each week and do what we can in the realm of heart and soul to imagine that life might be different somehow." What makes an astrological therapist anyway? Or, what does an astro-psychotherapist make? Serious students of both of these arts are on the increase. Maybe our correspondence is for them?

Love, Harte

October 6, 1987

Dearharte,

In your touching letter of 18 September, I was immediately struck by your question, "Can anyone willingly surrender?" I looked up the roots of the word and found the original meaning "to render up," and that immediately gave me images of supplication, of arms raised and hands cupped somewhat in a yielding, releasing gesture. (I just had an image of having nursed a bird with a broken wing back to health and having to let it go because its destiny is to fly.) I suspect such a gesture is not made at a time when all is going superbly well in one's life (somehow Oz and "Surrender, Dorothy!" come to mind), but rather is made when psyche has taken us some place, we've recognized the inevitabilities in that process, and we then have the choice either of fighting it (sometimes a good and noble fight) or surveying the terrain for a foundation, another road, or a launching pad. (One should also keep one's eye out for hobgoblins and quicksand as well.) In short, I don't think we take an option on surrender: it presents itself to us.

How does one hold any conscious sway in the realms of Neptune and Pluto anyway? I imagine you've heard out in California about the remarkable snowstorm we had here last Sunday. I awakened slowly that morning and through a slight opening in the curtains saw small, white "leaves" floating (albeit determinedly) down in front of the window. In that not quite-awake state my imagination led me to exclaim out loud, "My god! All the leaves have turned white—and they're all falling off the trees!" I got up, opened the curtains, and saw the ground covered with about eight inches of snow—my car half-buried by it. On 4 October! Since no snow plows were ready yet (many of them were buried in the snow). Nature had mandated a day of confinement, contemplation, and rest. Surrender. There was something much bigger and more important going on than could be accommodated by rational thought. I suspect that with a transiting Pluto opposite my Moon for the next two-plus years, I may have opportunities to learn about surrender; and I can't help wondering if that snowstorm was serving as a sort of Hermetic harbinger of what's in store for me in this place.

Your dream seems so timely here. My image of it has the canyon in front of us and the cone-shaped cave at our backs so that there's somehow no choice other than to go forward or back—no leisurely little toodle down the side of a hill after the day is spent. And does one ever go back, really? Joseph Campbell noted that, "Every time you cross the continent it's a totally different trip." So, in looking again into that dark matrix that contained us in our journey in your dream, we nonetheless look with eyes exposed to that same Leonine solar light that warmed our hands. But, isn't that what it's all about? What use to go back in as blind as the first time? Persephone's travails in the underworld turned her into "she who loves the darkness," and thus it is she who holds the lantern to light the way for all those of us who journey into Hades' realm.

Is there some moisture in that cave to slake the dry, dusty land on which you and I as astrological psychotherapists (translation: "star-speaking soul-healers") rest in your dream? Are there others in the cave whom we're to go and get and bring out into the light so that we can all explore the canyon? Since the cave is cone-shaped, and in anatomical terms I believe the "cone" is one of the cone-shaped cells in the retina of the eye sensitive to both color and intensity of light, is there more to this cave than meets the eye? (Caves are Saturn; eyes are the Sun; eyesight is Mercury.)

As is so with the dream, at this juncture, in my own odyssey east I'm more interested in what's in that cave than I am in exploring the canyon. I've been resident astrological psychotherapist at the school for six weeks, and it's already quite clear that transiting Saturn now on my Sun is going to pull me into that cave even as I struggle to stay in the light, even as I might also yearn to explore that canyon.

Toto, I have a feeling we're not in Kansas anymore.

Love, Hadley

PART 2

Star-Speaking Soul-Healers

Two of the unique Cosmic gifts given to humans are the ability of speech and the ability to form images.

-- Carol K. Anthony & Hanna Moog

I Ching: Oracle of the Cosmic Way

October 13, 1987

Hadley Dear Hadley,

If I'm late in answering forgive me. A heavy caseload coupled with a flu bug has left little time for anything else. I'm sorry your world is covered with snow this early in the season. That makes for a very long, sunless winter.

I've been getting together with a group of students, all astrologers in various phases of psychological education. Most of their questions center around the how-to of this work. Needless to say, these are the hardest questions to answer. I must admit that theoretical instruction, while often dull, triumphs over trying to convey the practical application of a phenomenological experience. I've been taping those sessions for my own study and am taking the liberty of enclosing a transcribed portion of our last session. Are there opportunities at your school to work in this way with any of the staff therapists?

Here it is:

John: Judie, has your work changed much since you incorporated psychotherapy into your astrological practice?

Judie: You bet. I've had to make certain considerations regarding the appropriate professional mix of astrology and psychotherapy. Overall the practice of both disciplines has deepened. I happen to feel it's just fine to allow astrology and psychotherapy to coexist openly, side by side when appropriate, even though each is really a very different experience with different goals. Psychotherapy traditionally provides an on-going or "working through" experience while, as you know, even one-time astrological consultation may present both astrologer and client with an entire gestalt of the client's core psychological issues. I know you can all attest to the incredible burst of affect or feeling which clients often demonstrate at an initial visit to their friendly neighborhood gypsy! And there are times when it just isn't appropriate to bring astrology into a therapy session. I think some kind of therapy or counseling, if you will, goes on automatically during any astrological consultation. Ultimately, it's the needs, mental status, and world view of the client that usually determine when and whether I mix the two disciplines. You folks will find your own level of comfort here, which will, I'm sure, be in keeping with the legal and ethical concerns of the area in which you practice.

Angela: The way the initial astrological consultation can be so psychologically therapeutic really fascinates me.

John: Sure, but ethically, legally, maybe even morally, we aren't yet equipped as astrologers to work in an ongoing way with the deeper feelings that get catalyzed in a client during that initial session.

Judie: And that's the point of this current educational process, to prepare you to do just that.

Angela: I feel excited, but a bit scared by the whole proposition. There's so much material to integrate. It feels overwhelming.

Judie: Listen, guys, there's no doubt that astrology has undergone a tremendous evolutionary process. It now extends right into the field of modern psychology. Historically, we've seen a shift from a traditional position that focuses on the reading of personal life events and esoteric possibilities to one which also might include the rich, mythic, astro-psychological ideas of Jungian analyst and astrologer, Liz Greene. The current literature more than substantiates the notion that astrology and psychotherapy have consummated a very noble marriage, one that's anything but barren. Just consider the works of Greene, of marriage and family counselor—and astrologer—Stephen Arroyo, Zip Dobyns, Ph.D. And those fine authors rest on the shoulders of more transpersonally-oriented brilliant folks like... .

John: Yes! The humanistic roots of thinkers like Dane Rudhyar, Marc Jones, and Noel Tyl! We're in great company here. But trying to synthesize it all and then apply it in a practical way therapeutically—yeah, that does feel overwhelming. And how do you know which method to practice? There's so much. Are we to be oracles, humanists, or mythologists?

Judie: I can't tell you when to bring Alice Bailey, Abraham Maslow, or Carl Jung into your consulting rooms. Don't limit yourselves by trying to fit your astro-psychological styles into tight little boxes or categories. You're aiming for the ability to move in and out of different astropsychological perspectives. Different occasions will call for different modes of interaction between yourselves and your clients. It's my belief that astrological psychotherapist and client may participate quite differently in each instance. The use of language and even of words may change with each session. The type of practices you have will also vary. You may have such a large psychotherapy practice that you only analyze an occasional horoscope. Or you may practice mainly astrology and refer clients out for therapy. From what I understand, Liz Greene works from a strict analytical model. She doesn't analyze the charts of her analysands. I do a bit of both: more therapy, less astrology.

Samuel: Jumping back a bit, how are you using the term "perspectives"?

Judie: Very flexibly. Are any of you familiar with James Hillman's *Re-Visioning Psychology*? I recommend it for anyone about to enter the field of psychology. I'm paraphrasing here, but Hillman refers to perspectives as modes, or forms of vision. He also uses the term "soul" to denote a "perspective rather than a substance." I understand this to mean that one must cultivate a kind of flexibility with clients. There must be a freedom of movement.

One must be present when doing psychological work. So, it doesn't really matter what mode you're in; that isn't the crucial thing. What matters is the psychological room you make in order to allow the psyche or soul to enter, to come into the session. I suggest you read Hillman and have your own experience of soul. Have we gone too far afield from your question of which method to practice, John?

John: No, actually not. These are very poetic notions. What you are really saying then, is that we mustn't forget Hermes (the astrological Mercury), the god who guides souls or soul, allowing him to enter and then to move.

Judie: So you see Hermes as the prime mover behind soul, or psyche. That's nice, I like that.

Angela: Judie, you mentioned the fertile marriage of astrology and psychotherapy. Following that metaphor then, what would you say astrology and psychotherapy give birth to?

Judie: I would say they bear or give birth to images. Images are born of the union of astrology and psychology. In my view, they're the offspring and central concern of both.

Hadley, after that meeting my head was filled with thoughts about astrology and psychotherapy. I had an urge to organize and contain these thoughts, while simultaneously feeling the need to let them fly free and uncontained.

I loved your thoughts on the cave dream. There are many others in that cave like John, Samuel, and Angela.

And I want to thank you for the answer to my question. Yes, astrological therapists are *star-speaking soul-healers.* They're like travelers on a parched, dry road strewn with rocklike "herms" which mark their way. Theirs is a thirst for imaginal waters to moisten the parched, dusty ground on which they rest. What do they seek? They seek images. I'm going back into that cave to look again. I don't know how long I'll be in there. I need to hear from you in the meantime.

J.

〰〰〰〰〰〰〰〰〰〰〰〰〰〰〰〰〰

22 October, 1987

Dear J,

So much has happened since I last wrote to you. Sorry to hear about your flu, and I sure hope you're feeling better—there's a vicious bug going around here, and it's felled a lot of children. Pray I don't get it.

I've had precious little time to adjust to life here, let alone to all that working at the school demands—and clearly will demand in exponential amounts—of me. If I'm to be honest, I imagine that I'm disconcerting myself with my unspoken agenda, my psychic "demands"/hopes/wishes for this system, in this system. I thank the gods daily for all my training in systems theory!

The transcription of dialogue with your astropsychology students couldn't have been more timely—boy, could I give them an earful! In addition to the myriad changes I'd not anticipated, I'll add another to the list: the change from private to institutional practice. Ye gods and goddesses! Coming out of private practice after all these years of autonomous Sagittarian functioning in that "sacred place" to which I referred in my first letter—coming out of that with all my circuits open and then walking into a system operating on a totally different ground within a totally different perspective (Hillman's definition is right on here) finds me on succeeding days (hours, minutes) either scrambling to fit a template of order over what I see as chaos, pulling the wagons into a circle, or rushing pell-mell to butt my head against the system's concrete wall. At this writing I don't think I could lead anyone out of your dream cave—I'm much too busy slipping on bat guano.

Ergo, in order to regain my footing, I've enlisted the help of a local Jungian therapist. As I subsequently phrased it to myself and her, I wanted her to help me stay centered in my inner world of archetypal reality while some very strange stuff in this system pulls at me from many directions. She has, thank god, agreed. People who work at the school can have therapy (at discount rates) with therapists who work at the school—not for moi. Boundaries, anyone?

When Adrian, the owner and executive director of the school, hired me this last spring, we were both excited about the possibilities inherent in introducing someone with my training, credentials, and experience in both astrology and psychotherapy into his private school. I so naively thought that because we were united in our conviction that working with a troubled kid necessitated working with the family system (families are required to participate actively in the children's treatment at the school,) we would, "of course," be united on a number of other basic fronts as well. The lesson for me here? ASSUME NOTHING.

Dear friend, how can I even begin to describe all that I see we must deal with as we bring this burgeoning field of astro-therapy into any kind of entrenched system, no matter how apparently "liberal"? Rather, how can I describe it in fewer than 100 pages at this writing? To be sure, many things about the school are atypical. Perhaps I'll write at length about that some other time—but all systems have certain traits in common; so it is my hope that I can add in absentia some fodder for your group's discussion. It occurs to me to go through my journal, make note of and annotate my entries heretofore regarding my experiences, impressions, and dreams. Perhaps that will help us both shine more light into the dark recesses of that cave.

I was immediately in some imaginal/imagined space here because I'd not been hired as a staff therapist with regular appointments and specific duties vis-à-vis the children or other staff and faculty members. Adrian said, "Tell me what you want to do here and how you think to do it, and I'll tell you if it's possible." Sounded good as the words wafted through the air between us. He introduced me very supportively to a number of faculty and staff people—I expected and got a mixed reaction, with the ratio of interest-to-scorn sufficiently in my favor; and he and I agreed that I'd begin my tenure there by doing a chart for any faculty or staff person who wanted one. That way, those who were working daily with the kids would have some experiential sense of what I do, could recommend the kids with whom, initially, it seemed most appropriate for me to work (the deeply troubled ones clearly out of the question) and we would evolve a method by which my astro-therapeutic work could find its way most productively into the system and into various treatment plans. (Incorrect Assumption #1: That there *are* treatment plans here.)

As this was all getting rolling, Adrian mailed an announcement to parents regarding my hiring, telling them I was a licensed therapist as well as astrologer, and assuring them that their child need have no contact with me if the family had an objection to astrology. Initial response from a few parents was surprisingly positive (will I ever be rid of this image of awakening some morning to find a cross burning on my lawn?) and I was really excited. Maybe my/our time had actually come! Then, "the letter" came: a three-page, single-spaced tirade at Adrian from an irate mother claiming astrology would give her son "another excuse for his appalling behavior"—a letter best synopsized under the rubric, "Are you out of your mind?? Don't let that woman near my son!"

For a moment or two I was a bit thrown (she was so angry and vitriolic) and then I saw it as an opportunity to face what we've known we're facing all along: the deadly combo of irrational fear and utter contempt which is based on lack of information. Do you, as I've done these many years, meet a new person or group and automatically assess for an instant whether you feel like running that gauntlet today/tonight? To wit, "Shall I tell them what I really do, or shall I put half of myself in the closet tonight and just tell them I'm a therapist?" Well, here I was faced with my promise to myself upon leaving LA: that I would never again cast my astrologer-self into the shadows for any reason.

So, assuming that a vindication of my hiring and my work was my responsibility (adult children of alcoholics are dynamos when it comes to responsibility), I sat up 'till the wee hours that night composing a thoughtful, intelligent, and, if I do say so, all 'round terrific apologia-cum-invitation to Mrs. (actually, "Dr.") X to engage in a dialogue with me about her concerns—the upcoming school open house being the perfect opportunity to meet and chat. Before sending it off, I thought I'd run it by Adrian so he'd know what I said if she came back at him. He looked at the two and one-half page letter, didn't read it, told me not to send it, and said I was just, "hooking into her stuff." I was dumbfounded! You can imagine the issues here—to list them and describe what went through my head would take pages more than I have time to type (though if it would be more instructive to your group, I can explain at a later date). Suffice it to say, I had a hard time acceding to Adrian's mandate; it just didn't feel right, but for various reasons I let it go. Three days later, an attorney for the student's divorced father sent a letter to the school saying how pleased he was to see that the school was enlightened enough to hire an astrologer to work with the kids. Go figure.

This entry from my journal is dated 29 September:

> A day of settling in, trying to figure out how/what I'm doing and going to do here. Listening to some of Richard (Idemon)'s last tapes helps me to get back on track, but there's an enormous challenge to introduce this whole level of material into a system that worships at the shrine of Fritz Perls (Gestalt therapy is IT)—no sense of how yet at all. The kids touch me deeply and repeatedly, though, and I find myself almost wishing they didn't. These struggling souls are seen by all around me so differently from how I see them. Staff burn-out rate very high here. What's that about?

Every day I attend a "therapists' lunch," where all of the school therapists, the resident psychiatrist (who hasn't the faintest idea whether to laugh or cry about me) and head honchos eat and discuss what's going on with various kids. Confidentiality doesn't exist here, and I have relentless difficulty with that. There is no "sacred place," no container, no safe haven or final arbiter for the contents of a child's soul. Anything a kid says to anyone, anytime, in a therapy session or out, is fair game for discussion with anyone involved with the school—the rationale being that "secrets" are not in the child's best interests. You and I with our family systems training know this is so in a number of contexts, but my argument here is that confidentiality—forging that crucible of trust which makes imagining a different life possible—is the sine qua non of the therapeutic/healing process, not to mention a legal mandate in California. Without the Saturnian limits, how can Uranian chaos and Neptunian spectres lead but to madness? The soul, for lack of boundaries, sees only the abyss and becomes a prisoner of its own fear—all these planets are, after all, in a solar system.

When I brought up the issue of the necessity for boundaries (can you imagine the very horror of life without Saturn?) in a discussion with Adrian, he dismissed me with an angry, "There are no boundaries here!" When I went, in a state of profound upset, to one of the heads of the therapy department, I was told I'd have to let go of all my "private practice stuff" and that "the kids get used to it being this way." I'm sure people get used to the K.G.B. too, but what does it do to their souls? There's a whiff of cultishness in all this. It's terribly disconcerting and already might bode ill for my future here. I'm beyond grateful I decided not to accept campus housing. Living a few miles away is proving to be very important.

In Mycenae, Greece, the palace where Agamemnon met his end is surrounded by what are called "Cyclopean" walls—walls made of stones so large it's believed that only a Cyclops could have put them there; it's impossible to imagine how they would ever be moved. I have the feeling/image of being both closed-in and shut-out by Cyclopean walls. I fear getting stuck battling the system (natal Uranus and Saturn opposing my Sun), not knowing how much is too much compromise, even for the chance to do this work I love and which I hope to have others learn to value and use. I find both positive and negative manifestations of the Saturn archetype permeating my thoughts. Weariness seeps in through my pores.

I recorded a dream the night of that snowstorm earlier this month—actually I think it was a series of dreams in which crowds were everywhere. I was trying to find my way through them—to find my place, my seat; I was getting lost, looking for an address. At one point in some kind of assembly hall with tables and chairs, I looked over at a place on the "second floor." Adrian was watching me—no affect—just watching me. The feelings around this were primarily of frustration rather than fear or anything else.

Through all of this, I do have the good fortune to return each night to the sanctuary of this lovely little house in the country—my container, my sacred place. What worries me is that I return utterly exhausted, with no time or energy for my reading or spiritual practices—no time to do what feeds my soul. I trust this won't go on forever once I hit my stride, catch my rhythm in the system.

The good news is that I attended the first "full faculty" meeting (therapists, teachers, and staff) earlier this month and really liked so many of the people I'll be working with. Shortly after that, I met with one of the therapy directors, and we had something of a meeting-of-the-minds re how I might organize my work here. However, honesty requires me to say that the opportunity to prove how deftly I could walk on egg shells was quite present. She clearly doesn't like me, but she doesn't hate me either, so let's take the glass as half full.

On 10 October there was a school open house with parents coming from all over. I had very good, enthusiastic contact with a number of parents who seemed more than willing to cooperate in upcoming group family therapy weekends where I'll get to demonstrate the use of astrology as a way of approaching issues and dynamics in the family system (now that's part of the dream come true.)

I have a great deal more to tell you if I'm to catch you up on my "initiation"—the "purifying fire" given new meaning here. I fear I've gone on much too long already, but if you're interested, next time I'll tell you about having taken on one of the "hopeless" kids, working with him "my" way (I was brought here to do that, lest we forget), and the repercussions that work is beginning to have in the system. Old Fritz is doing nip-ups in his grave.

As you know, the school has a branch further south; Adrian wants me to go at the end of this month so I can begin to set up my work there—another new system to enter. Is that Hades I hear laughing?

Thanks for reading through all this—and love,

Hadley

~~~~~~~~~~~~~~~~~~~~~~~~~~~~~~~~

November 6, 1987

Dearest Hadley,

What a heart-wrenching letter. Your initial experiences at the school sound so disappointing. I felt your disillusionment to the very core of my being. If this were a telegram instead of a letter, the next few lines would probably read:

> Hadley: They (the children) need you. Stop. Don't go for the politics. Go for the images. Stop. Your work with astro-psychological images can effect the children's patterns of behavior. Stop. You will have an impact. Stop.

Yes, I know exactly what you mean when you say you fear finding an "astro-cross" (my term) burning on your lawn. I'll fess up: the "societal"/collective shame of being identified as an "astrologer" haunts me. This astrologer often still hides out in her closet—wrapped shamefully in a cloak of family therapy. However, what I know and what I own, is that it's the Ku Klux Klan within myself of which—or is it witch?—I'm so ashamed and with which I'm so uncomfortable. Those inner, devilish, fire-carrying, disowned figures within my own psyche, with soul-less slits for eyes, on occasion still brand me a charlatan, a fake. I believe this issue of astrological authenticity is one which most conscious astrologers and astro-psychotherapists have an ethical obligation to confront. Once we can honestly claim and acknowledge these demons within ourselves I believe we'll be closer to standing proudly by our art. I'm doing better all the time.

I hope you will see my mock telegram as bringing moral support. It is not without sympathy or empathy for your valid systemic concerns. It's just that my personal bias leans toward changing systems on a small, rather than a large scale. The political murkiness of Adrian's organization sounds overwhelming. I was especially struck by the lack of respect for the kids' privacy. I'm convinced your best work will be done with the adolescents individually and within their family context. I'm most eager to receive a blow-by-blow account of what, I suspect, will be terribly innovative work on your part. I'd love a sample of astrological method as it blends psychologically with family systems. I realize tape recordings might be off limits, but perhaps you could, as they say, "wear a wire"?!

I have been spending time in "our" cave. I continue to muse over endless questions and thoughts about astrology, especially as it has developed and combined with various psychological traditions. In addition to its compatibility with Humanistic and Jungian Psychology, I believe there is yet another way in which astrological method and practice may combine with psychological thought. I go 'round and 'round with these fantasies, but these ideas (Mercury) are still in thought form and seem to resist congealing, or as they say in alchemical symbolism, coagulating into something solid

(Saturn). Inner voices continually try to attack and undermine my ideas. Inside my head I hear those critical questions like, "What do you think you're doing? Let go of your crazy, inflated notions and come down to earth."

I could reduce this inner rap to the nasty critique of the Jungian negative animus, that inner, contrasexual masculine voice within a woman which, instead of guiding her to a more enlightened psychological position, often only degrades her attempts at fulfillment and self-improvement. In an effort to make him more conscious, I could take on the protests of this challenging, unconscious inner voice by engaging him in that Jungian process of active imagination. *Or* I could turn to dialogue with the images themselves for help. By viewing them as imaginal figures within my psyche I will perhaps be able to confront and be challenged by them and even get to know them better. Could it be that these new images of psyche and horoscope ask only for a safe, psychological landscape in which to incarnate? At the very least they deserve the responsible attentions of a Scorpio midwife. I figure I owe them a secure, comfortable birthing center filled with warm, life-giving waters. I don't know what I'll do, but I do know it's time to get off the stick. I'll keep you posted.

I'll sign off by returning again to Hillman and his thoughts of the heart, which is where this correspondence began. I know it must feel right now like you're in a barren desert, but as Hillman notes, the desert is only barren "once we desert the heart." If, as Hillman has described, it is "the passions of the soul" which make the desert habitable," and if "the desert is where the lion lives," then if you wish to keep your lion fed, you must follow the passions of your soul.

Hadley, that is one hungry lion. I can hear her roar way out here on the west coast. Know, dear friend, that I am with you every step of the way.

With love, Judie

~~~~~~~~~~~~~~~~~~~~~~~~~~~~~~

12 November 1987

Dear Friend,

Your thoughtful, supportive letter was waiting for me when I returned from my initiatory visit to Adrian's other school. Do keep those imaginal telegrams and letters coming in! I left this northern enclave shortly after my last letter to you and found myself immediately in another world, different climate, architecture (clearly I've never given sufficient thought to the images and energies conjured by differences in architecture), a new staff with very different "rhythms" (engendered, one might imagine, by tropical breezes versus having to bundle and bend against the blizzard), and a whole new set of kids and families. The good news is that I felt an almost palpable openness to my work from the moment I landed. The resident psychiatrist there made a point of stopping to chat with me, and I was thrilled to find that he shared my frustration at the lack of a Bodhi Tree Bookstore anywhere but in L.A.!

But before I draw you into my experiences there, let me backtrack so I can orient you to what was happening here. As I indicated, I'd met with Doreen, one of the therapy directors, and developed a preliminary m.o. to be tried and modified as we go along. In short, whenever I do an astrological analysis for one of the children, I'm to do it in a lengthy therapy session with the child's therapist (each student has one) present. That way the therapist doesn't have to listen back to each student's tape of the session, and I can confer with the student and therapist simultaneously regarding my astrological portrait of the student's personal and family dynamics.

My thought here is that my analysis can perform a number of functions:

1. Point up the key intrapsychic and interfamilial dynamics/issues in the chart for long-term therapeutic follow-up—especially for newer students and/or those who are having trouble articulating their own issues;

2. Discover previously unrecognized patterns (which I believe astrology does particularly well)—especially helpful for kids from highly dysfunctional families where the need to idealize Mom and Dad in order to avoid the gut-wrenching pain of reality keeps the child in self-deprecating denial;

3. Facilitate the use of images, telling of stories, myths, etc., to help the children reconceptualize their issues and dilemmas in a way that stays with them visually and emotionally. This generation is not populated with readers, and their developmental tasks don't

necessarily embrace the understanding of the psychological constructs underlying their behavior;

4. Synopsize the issues as seen through the chart so that the therapist and child who've worked together for a longer period of time can assess progress and have, I would hope, a reinforcing feeling of accomplishment.

As you know, my initial sessions here were done mostly with faculty and staff to give them a sense of my work. The theory behind doing that makes sense. In real life ... well, here again is that word "overwhelm" which I suspect you'll be seeing a lot vis-à-vis my experiences in these letters. The image I have is of myself standing at the edge of the ocean; I know I have to dive in and swim somewhere, and that's O.K. because I'm a good swimmer, and the day is beautiful.

Then, off to my left, clouds begin to gather, the sky changes quickly, the ocean starts to rumble, and it's as if Walter Crane's painting "The Horses of Neptune" has come to life. Do you know the painting? I can't actually see the horses, but I feel the "shore-shaker" attributes of Poseidon/Neptune. (Transiting Neptune is just past the conjunction to my natal Mercury and is squaring natal Neptune.) There's no place to run or retreat (the horses coming out of the ocean would trample me on shore); my only hope is to dive into the water and try to swim against their power or with it or through it.

That image presents itself as I experience and reflect on my sessions with the staff—the people who are *in charge* of the kids: some of them seem rather "untherapized," seem to need as much (if not more) help than the children! A lot of dysfunctional family of origin stuff being replicated. There's no point in going into the details and ramifications of that here—I think the image speaks for itself and certainly addresses your admonishing me to focus on "changing systems on a small scale rather than a large scale." Maybe the key is to jump on the back of one of those horses and ride for all I'm worth!

So, let me get back to a reference at the end of my last letter regarding my beginning to work with one of the "hopeless" kids—let's call him Denny Smith. I first saw Denny in the dining hall one evening when Adrian was in a pique and had launched into one of his diatribes on some issue. Rather quickly it became evident that Adrian was directing his invective at a particular student, speaking of having been personally betrayed, "abused" (a favorite word around here) and let down by someone whom he'd taken under his wing and that this experience had made him question whether he wanted to keep the school going or even to continue doing this work. (Oh, the drama!)

Well, I couldn't imagine what sort of mighty and powerful being could've brought Adrian to this edge of histrionic rage, and at that point he announced he was "giving up on Denny Smith." Everyone turned to the table next to me to stare; and while the intensity of the excoriation had created for me the image of a monster-child-perpetrator of heinous crimes, the image I actually saw was that of a small, sweet-looking, sloe-eyed child of about 15, whose soul appeared to have left his body slumped in something quite beyond humiliation—like a puppy utterly unable to comprehend why he'd been whipped this much. I remember gasping audibly while the "old-timers" seemed to take it all in stride and further isolated him by shaking their heads knowingly.

Dinner ended and everyone went on about their business, but I couldn't stop wondering about this kid. I asked around about him and heard quite a number of horror stories about drug addiction, lying, theft, and masterful manipulation. "He's very seductive," "He's a pro," I was told, "Everybody's tried to help him—he's just no good." (Has no one contemplated the role of the scapegoated child in a family system??)

The next day was a special "off campus" day for the children who were divided into small groups and assigned to us adults to be taken in our cars wherever we would agree to go for the afternoon. Do you believe in Fate, that Moira (pronounced "meer-a") of Greek myth, over whom even Zeus has no power? I have such a small car that only two children were assigned to me: one of them was Denny Smith! Walking toward me, this miscreant who had brought 47-year-old Adrian to his knees was so little!

I'll spare you the details of the afternoon; suffice it to say that Denny introduced himself and then said he was so excited when he found out that he was in my car because he'd heard about the astrologer on campus and wanted to meet me. The twin flags—"masterful manipulator," and "a pro"—went up. But as the afternoon unfolded quietly, he talked like a 15-year-old kid who knew he was in a lot of trouble. At times it sounded like a rap to draw me in—he asked good questions about astrology, described his complex relationship with Adrian. At other times he was clearly quite narcissistically disconnected; at still other times, he was utterly ingenuous. As he got out of the car, he thanked me, walked away with his friend, and then turned around and asked me how he could "sign up" with me. I told him what birth data I needed, and it just so happened that his mother was coming to school for a parent-therapist-teacher conference that next weekend.

Shortened long story: I got birth data for the whole family from a weary, desperate, puzzled mother who had just flown in and wasn't at all eager to talk with me. I did Denny's chart that night and sent the rest of the data to the computer service. I was particularly interested in the connections between his chart and mine—I'm sure you've noticed how important and helpful this can be with certain clients.

Interesting. Here was this child now so singled out for isolation from the system (the ultimate punishment), I looked at his chart with four planets and two asteroids in Libra in the seventh house along with Pluto and the asteroid Juno. Counter to all this is the Moon conjunct Chiron in Aries in the first house. Well, with all that Libran need for relatedness, why wouldn't he develop very narcissistic defenses as a way of nurturing himself when he couldn't connect? Isolating him and publicly humiliating him was not going to "bring him around" by any means. Also, the school deals with the children so relentlessly in the context of a group process, peer pressure, etc., that when you factor in his Capricorn-ruled 11th house ruled by a retrograde Saturn in the third, and the lack of boundaries in the system, this is a kid who really can learn to play the game like a pro while (no squares) he never develops any internal sense of who he might really be or become.

So, since Adrian had given me "carte blanche" to find my way to work in the system, and since Denny had, in the following two days, so thoroughly transgressed that he was confined to his dorm for the foreseeable future, I decided to take him on. I wanted to see what I could do using his chart as a jumping-off point and spending an hour daily in one-on-one session with him. The image I held was that of a very sad little boy who'd been given a very large, colorful court jester costume that dwarfed him. But every time he said or did what the "audience" or the "court" or the "king" wanted him to do, the costume seemed to fit him a little better—as if he magically stretched himself into the costume somehow and could thus pretend it fit. Yet when he was away from the group and by himself, he was still a sad, bewildered little boy in this huge costume, feeling more awkward than ever and withdrawing more and more into himself for protection.

I worked with Denny for a couple of weeks this way, talked to him a lot about all the parent-child psychodynamics I saw in his chart, his parents' marriage, their parents, and what it meant to be the child of an alcoholic parent (no one had ever addressed this in therapy!). I put in the simplest terms possible what I just astrologically "shorthanded" to you above. I also busted him more than once for trying to con me and warned him that if he kept trying to do that, I wouldn't come back. Now, I'm not so naive as to fail to recognize the inflation that comes with the first rush of this "call to adventure." He'd seem to get very connected to me with all this attention and then just shut down. However, I kept calling up Schwartz-Salant's concept of the narcissistic wound (a powerful image for me), and that kept me from turning off when he would absolutely check out on me at times. George his dorm proctor came and hugged me early in the third week; he felt Denny was really beginning to make some progress that George could trust. He said he'd personally never truly given up on this kid and would be glad to work with me in any way I wanted. I was so grateful because I was getting exhausted with this intense hour every day, plus all my other scheduled sessions with children and staff. Also, while every one in the school knew what I was doing, no one but George had offered support, or even said anything at all to me—that is, until ....

In the middle of the third week Denny's therapist Mick stopped me on the grounds and said that, while he saw my "good intentions," he wanted to warn me that "the minute you turn your back, this kid will stick a knife in it." I was dumbstruck! I collected myself, drew a breath, and agreed that may be a possibility, but that I felt I had enough ego strength to withstand a clinical "betrayal" by a 15-year-old boy! Then, lest he think I was "just" an astrologer, my ACA self had to show that I did, indeed, have clinical chops. So I proceeded to explain that I wasn't really working strictly from either Kernberg's or Kohut's "model" for narcissism and that I'd been finding Schwartz-Salant to be the most helpful, to wit: "The issues raised by the narcissistic character disorder are those of the suffering and the depths of the soul."[6]

I watched Mick's face go blank: Ohmygod! He had never heard of any of these people! He looked at me, narrowed his eyes to your KKK "soul-less slits," and reiterated: "I'm telling you this kid's gonna get you." And he walked away. I figured I must be doing something right if he was that upset.

The next day I went to see Denny for our morning session and then sat in on a group dorm session in which he actually seemed to connect with a couple of the other kids more than once—and without his jester suit. George caught my eye and smiled. Then, I went to the usual therapists' lunch. I had indeed been "following the passions of my soul," and that had "made the desert habitable."

But I was unaware that I was about to be fed to the lions ...

Therapists gave reports on their various kids and then at the end of lunch Doreen pulled herself up to her full height and turned to me from across the room to say: "And I'm warning you, Hadley, to back off with Denny Smith. You're spending too much time with him—he's begun to see you as some sort of goddess (her words). He's very seductive, and you're going to find yourself in a lot of trouble. You're not to see him any more."

[6] Schwartz-Salant, Nathan. *Narcissism and Character Transformation: The Psychology of Narcissistic Character Disorders*, Inner City Books, Toronto, Canada, 1982, p.28

Well, how can I describe what I felt? What's the image? Vultures hovering high because "it's not carrion yet"? Who had told me about who stabbing me in the back? Every eye in the room was on me. I swear, my heart rate felt like it was 250—easy. I took a deep breath, looked at Doreen, and said, "I'm 43 years old. I've been a clinician for ten years, and I'm good at what I do. I'm quite capable of dealing with the seductive manipulations of a narcissistic 15-year-old boy. I am, however, baffled as to how this child managed to get so much power in this system." (This lion was not going to roll over and play dead, though there was at this moment a dead silence. Hmmm. Perhaps the system was in danger of losing its Identified Patient?) Doreen The Undaunted said, "And I'm telling you to back off."

It was a Friday. I went, exhausted, to New York City for the weekend, had a wonderful visit with an old friend from "the outside," and came back to work that Tuesday. George ran up to me before the morning faculty meeting and asked if I'd heard about Denny yet. My heart sank to my paws (this is about hearts, you know). He said that Denny had packed his bag and was getting ready to run away with two other kids Sunday night. The two kids took off, but Denny had come to George's room around 3:00 a.m. crying and saying that he didn't really want to run away, that he wanted to get his life together. Then George said, "I think you should know that Denny told me the main reason he didn't run away was because of what you'd done for him." I was glad I had Kleenex in my purse; I hate crying first thing in the morning.

This was the week before I left to go south. I had a lot of work to do and was grateful to feel able to ease up on the amount of time spent with Denny and likewise grateful to feel rather vindicated in sticking with my astrotherapeutic approach. No one, other than George, said another word—positive or negative—to me about Denny (though everyone knew he'd been close to running away). When I put his chart next to Adrian's, I saw how he stirs up Adrian's old issues with his own mother—some really deep counter-transference stuff going on there all along—but "the boss" (in whom I'm beginning to see strains of BPD and gods-only-know what else) is still too angry at this child to be approached about his own issues in this relationship, so I'll save that insight for another time.

On 28 October I was packing to fly south and felt this awful virus all the kids have creeping ever deeper into my body—guess my immune system is really under siege. Truly didn't want to fly; wanted to crawl into bed and sleep for days. The trip to New York made me realize how much I feel like an expatriate here—no one speaks my language, or nourishes my soul. I'm so grateful for my friends in the city and on the coast—for you especially, dear Scorpio-midwife friend.

The night before I left I had this dream: I met a man who lived on 53rd Avenue, in Seattle (the street on which I lived until age six when we moved to California.) When I looked closely at what he was doing, I saw that he was slitting open the hide of a stag.

The stag is a symbol of renewal, creation, fire, the dawn. J.C. Cooper says "The stag at enmity with the chthonic serpent, like the warring eagle and serpent, represents the conflict of opposites, positive versus negative, light against darkness, etc. The stag trampling the serpent underfoot is the victory of spirit over matter, good over evil."[7] In Greek myth, the stag is the symbol of Artemis. If I had time, I'd have a long dialogue with the stag in that dream. A quote came to my attention recently: "What is to give light must endure burning."

Yours, let us pray, in the light,
Hadley

---

[7] Cooper, J.C. *An Illustrated Encyclopedia of Traditional Symbols*, London, Thames and Hudson, 1978, p.158

PART 3

On Reimagining

I later learned that symbols and myths work in that way; they grab one's psyche suddenly and fill it with ideas as well as with energy.

-- Michael Meade, *Fate and Destiny:
The Two Agreements of the Soul*

November 25, 1987

Dear Hadley,

It was great talking with you on the phone. A rare occurrence these days. Our conversation yielded a great gift. When you called I was so excited to hear from you I forgot to turn off my answering machine after I picked up; it's an ancient one, and the tape doesn't automatically stop, so most of our conversation was recorded. I now have those elusive ideas relative to astro-psychotherapy in concrete form. Together we've animated them. Once again you've played the part of facilitator in my life. Here for posterity, is your transcribed copy of the significant parts of our call:

J: Hadley! What great timing—I was just answering your letter. When I got to that passage about your imagined race with Crane's "Horses of Neptune," I said out loud: "Why doesn't she just get on the back of one of those bloody horses and ride?" A few phrases later I saw you'd arrived at the same conclusion.

H: I'm hanging on to that horse's mane for dear life. This is really a life-altering experience for me.

J: So I've gathered from your letters. They're so poetic, yet so painfully restrained. I loved your reference to Crane's painting. It's one of my favorites.

H: No kidding!

J: No, your thoughts on it generated some surprisingly significant metaphors. Can you imagine daring to out-race those horses? Jump on their backs, yes; try to out-race them, forget it. Do you suppose those beautiful beasts are the imaginal messengers of the sea god Neptune, the mythological Poseidon?

H: I do, yes. Those horses seem to me to do more than emerge out of the ocean.

J: It's as if they're the body of the ocean and at the same time they're evolving into the crashing waves.

H: And Neptune…. He seems to drive those horses with all the psychic energy available to any person or beast in any given moment. What mythic dimension do you think his horses represent? Don't you suppose he's the Father of Dreams in a certain realm? That he fathers some particular aspect of dreams?

J: Interesting, isn't it, how the gods embody different aspects of the mythic world within us. So, if we take Hades/Pluto as fathering dreams in the underworld realm, then Neptune/Poseidon could very well father another dimension of the dream world. "Sea Father of Dreams," I think that title suits him. And I think those wild, beautiful horses are the messengers that carry our dreams, images, fantasies.

H: So the messages the horses deliver are like forms of psychic energy that ascend out of unconscious waters into consciousness.

J: Exactly! In the painting Neptune/Poseidon is the driver— the force—the prime mover behind those images...

H: Am I confused?

J: Stay with me here while we pursue the metaphor. If we take the horses as the messengers of psyche's images, then to ride that horse for all it's worth would be like making a commitment to follow that imaginal horse until the images that he carries have been fully revealed.

H: Well, right now it sure takes more courage to ride an imaginal horse than a real one!

J: Sure, but what's the alternative?

H: Probably to abandon the imaginal reality that moves you (that horse). But then you desert the passions of your soul, and you compromise your faith in the reality of the images that stirred your soul to begin with—heavy consequences.

J: "Faith" is an important term there; it takes a special kind of faith to pull this off.

H: How do you mean?

J: Do you know the term "psychological faith"?

H: No.

J: I have a piece from Hillman right here: "The work of soul-making is concerned essentially with the evocation of psychological faith, the faith arising from the psyche which shows as faith in the reality of the soul. Since psyche is primarily image and image always psyche, this faith manifests itself in the belief in images." He goes on, but that gives you the gist of it.

H: I like that. It's helpful, too, especially when I think of the initial panic I usually feel when faced with a client's dream. Do you ever experience that?

J: All the time. It's hard to admit because "we in this profession" aren't supposed to feel at a loss for psychological answers! When I hear a dream these days, if I translate it into astrological language I gain a much quicker access to psyche's messages! But then speed in these matters isn't always the goal!

H: I've learned that at first I draw a blank, but if I stay with that sense of the unknown and trust the dream image—work with it long enough—slowly, the dream images do reveal themselves and begin to transform. I'll have to try doing more astrological translation myself. There's such a compatibility between the psyche's messages and the language of the horoscope.

J: Sometimes I think that's only because astrology is the one universal symbolic language which I happen to be so familiar with. But whatever the reason, I'm glad for it. You know, we haven't had one of our "real" talks for so long—it's great—but it's your dime so I want to be conscious of time and money, both difficult subjects for the soul.

H: Before we hang up I'm curious to know how you're relating all this to linking astrology with psychotherapy.

J: If anyone would know this, it would be you. We've both felt something to be missing from the work we do for some time now. I've felt that astrological psychotherapy, even in its current fullness, can still be extended to include something else.

H: Such as?

J: An imaginal approach.

H: O.K., I'm with you, but how are you using the term "imaginal"?

J: By imaginal, all I really mean is the incorporation of an image-focused approach into the astro-psychotherapeutic setting.

H: That's all?

J: I don't think it's necessary to get too complicated here with sophisticated definitions. After all I'm using that term to describe an additional method of working with psychological astrology. There are many who have written eloquently about the philosophical, transpersonal, artistic, and psychological dimensions of imaginal space. It seems rather absurd to simplify it in this way, yet the process of attending to images can be so rich and so deep that once you participate in that process, you're immediately in a depth psychological mode.

H: My guess is that working imaginally could wed a depth psychological experience to the astro-psychological encounter. We'd work less with astrological jargon and more with images related to the client's concerns.

J: Yes. After all the horoscope is analyzed metaphorically.

H: And those metaphors are generators of images.

J: This is exciting!

H: So the equation would be image = psyche = horoscope.

J: Yes!

H: Do you remember that wonderful piece by Charles Poncé, where he refers to astrology as an imaginal art?

J: Of course, "Saturn and the Art of Seeing" in his essay collection. Have you ever heard him speak?

H: Yes! He's a wonderful weaver of the mythic and the psychological. I think his ideas about a new astrology are marvelous.

J: Truly! If you could get astrologer and client working together to imagine or create a new mythology relevant to the client's life ...

H: It would work beautifully. But, one last question: What's the method for an image-focused approach?

J: One last question? We'll be here for days! The method would be an experiential, mutual process of imaginal dialogue. The astrologer, or as in this case, astro-psychotherapist and client might be like two explorers engaging in a process of mutual discovery.

H: This conversation will overflow into tomorrow if we get into that one tonight!

J: There's so much more here. You just don't know how much more creative and improvisational the work has become since I've begun to include, albeit tentatively, this imaginal approach. And you know, it's curious how working this way has stimulated me to trace the different ways in which astrology has become psychological. It's as if there are different styles, or modes of psychological astrology. Astrology combines with Humanistic and Jungian psychology, but if you were to put these styles or modes into actual categories, you'd have to begin with astrology itself as a non-psychological mode of counseling.

H: And then ...?

J: And then the Humanistic approach would follow.

H: And the Jungian approach would follow that.

J: Yes, and each mode or perspective would focus on a different concern.

H: Right. The traditional mode of astrological counseling would focus on events.

J: The Humanistic on the person, and the Jungian would focus on meaning.

H: Then of course, we'd add the imaginal approach which focuses on images.

J: I've been thinking of organizing this material more formally. What do you think?

H: I think it's a great idea. Why don't you present it to your group? They could use it as study material for discussion. Should be right up their alley.

J: That's a great idea. It would bring the material to life. Thanks for the suggestion.

H: Do you have any case material from the imaginal work you've done so far in your practice?

J: I'm just beginning to gather some, and is it ever fascinating.

H: If you can get permission from your clients, I'd love to see it.

J: As soon as I have it I'll get it to you. But just think—I finally had the guts tonight to climb on that sea stallion's back, and he led me into what you and I just explored together. More than anything, right now in this moment, I want to savor that.

H: Me too ….

~ ~ ~ ~ ~ ~ ~ ~ ~ ~ ~ ~

I realize I didn't mention it enough during our conversation, so I'll tell you to get it in writing. That work you did with "Denny Smith" was outstanding. I keep re-reading your written descriptions of him. They are so eloquent. And your clinical work, very impressive.

Another thing: your dream about the "wound" in the hide of the stag. It occurred to me that "stag" is also a name for the state of being single, i.e. stag party. I'm not sure why, but I feel a dialogue with that stag would be most revealing to you at this point in time. I also connect Artemis, a very *single* goddess, with Sagittarius. Needless to say, J.C. Cooper's amplifications of the word 'stag' bear a close resemblance to those states of soul in which you've been living, of late.

Good night, and keep the "faith."

Heartsie (a name given to me by my twin Sagittarian nephews)

~~~~~~

4 December 1987

Dear Heartsie, (I like it!)

This letter will be shorter than the last one. I'm about to head back to the southern campus again, as Adrian is concerned (at *this* moment, anyway) that the parents and students down there get an equal amount of my attention.

I'm so glad that phone call got recorded! I never would've remembered all that. When we talked about facing a client's dream the first time (interesting idea, "facing a dream," like Hillman's *Facing the Gods*?) you mentioned translating a dream into astrological language in order to gain quicker access to psyche's messages. Seeing that piece of our conversation on paper, I realize that I just let it go by without probing for more details. Consider this a probe. Do you have any clinical examples that you have permission to discuss?

You're quite right that a dialogue with that stag in the dream I reported to you last time would probably be most revealing. I think there's a key to the dream's message in your colloquial association of the word "stag" with the state of being single. In my current environment that state has a quality of woundedness about it, as does, I think, the whole domain of the feminine here.

Heretofore I've made a pretty full life in my unsought state as "Hadley Parthenia" these many years. But I realize the dream is telling me that since I've been here I've been feeling more and more like "Hadley Eviscerata": few opportunities to contain and collect the self, and perhaps too many to be ripped open and have the insides (the heart?) removed. That the man in the dream was related to my childhood home probably has to do with psyche's (Poseidon's?) message. Some energy similar to that at work in my childhood is operative here and I'm not yet conscious of it. Who knows?

However, when I read your suggestion about dialoguing with the stag, I was acutely conscious of how little time there is in my life for anything of the kind these days. And I have more than a little concern about what will happen if this pace has to be kept indefinitely. What happens to the well-being of one's soul/heart when the images that have nourished it are given no room in which to roam around? When their "place" is taken from them the way Fascists proscribe the freedom of movement in a people? What happens when we are so assaulted by what's "out there" that we have no time to generate anything from within? Yet another reason why I'm so appreciative of this particular connection with you, my friend.

And speaking of what happens to images, I had a remarkable experience with a student on that first trip south in October, and it seems quite germane here. Within a few hours after I'd arrived on the campus Adrian swooped past me—he does a lot of swooping—and said to all attendant ears, "Give him to Hadley. Let's see if *she* can do anything with him. I'm sick of this!" (I had a feeling this wasn't quite akin to winning the lottery.) And into my life walked a boy I'll call "Paco." He's definitely older than the other boys, stringy lean, pock-marked face with haunted eyes and a sort of smile that doesn't know where to go. Somehow he was pacing even when he was standing still. He was told to sit and wait while I was filled in on his background—my being yet another person, I soon learned, to be filled in on Paco's background.

His adoptive parents were originally from two different countries and travel a lot. He'd been at the school for over three years, had great difficulty relating to other kids, could be violent, seemed bright but learning-disabled, would make progress, get close to graduating, and then sabotage himself. I asked if there was any battering or alcoholism in the family; the proctor didn't know. I asked to see the clinical file and was met with, "Oh God, it's an inch thick—he's been tested by everybody for everything, but he's on meds now and that seems to calm him down." I decided I'd read the file later and asked what the immediate problem was. "Oh, he's just acting crazy again," said the proctor.

I was told I could see him for as long as I wanted, and I said I wanted a quiet room somewhere. We were taken to the faculty house, and I was told not to let him walk back to the main building by himself. I looked over at Paco and found myself trying not to be naively unafraid of him. Something in his eyes looked scared, not scary. (Do you realize how the word "scared" changes if you switch the positions of the "a" and the "c?")

We sat on the group room floor. I turned on the tape recorder that I'm now determined to use when I see students alone. I asked him for his birth date and sketched out a solar chart from the ephemeris just to get a bit of information. He was very tense, restless, and I asked what he thought about when he saw me put those symbols on that wheel. He said, "I think you'll try to help me." He has the Sun in Sagittarius and Moon in Capricorn. I saw the Mercury-Neptune conjunction in Scorpio and Uranus conjunct Pluto in Virgo, and thought there must be some pretty intense stuff bottled up in that psyche, some of it probably labeled "pathological" in that inch thick file. Since all the psychiatric folks had apparently had their go at him, I felt oddly free to give his demons (if that's what they turned out to be) a place to come out and stretch. People were coming and going outside, so I could call for help if I had to.

I asked what happened inside him when he really got angry. He was quiet, checking me out for a moment. Then, pointing to his heart(!) he said, tentatively, that he felt like something wild was walking back and forth there. He kept circling a small area with his finger. I said it looked like that wild thing was in some kind of a cage. His face lit up, and he said, "Oh, she is!" I asked what kind of a "she" we were talking about, and he instantly said, "La Tigressa." I asked if anyone at the school knew about La Tigressa, and he said, "No, they'd all think I was crazy." I asked if he ever talked to her, and he looked at me doubtfully; I said I wouldn't think he was crazy if he talked with her. He said she wasn't allowed to say much, and I asked if that was because of the cage (I was looking at the Saturn/Uranus opposition in his chart.) He thought for a moment; I saw in his face that he was trying to be "logical" here, and I didn't want that to interfere with the image. I broke in with the idea that if she couldn't speak and was in a cage, perhaps there was a zookeeper; I asked him to close his eyes and see if there was a zookeeper anywhere around. He said he saw one—in a uniform—dressed like a soldier (Saturn in Aries!). Our exchange went like this:

H: Does he have a gun?

P: No. He has keys.

H: Ah, so he could open the cage if he wanted to?

P: Yes, but he's afraid.

H: Of what?

P: That she'll run away.

H: And hurt someone?

P: No. Just run away, go away.

H: Does the zookeeper ever talk to her?

P: He'd like to, but he doesn't think she'd understand.

H: Does he know how she feels sometimes?

P: Oh yes. He knows exactly how she feels.

This was so encouraging, Judie! Paco was calm, his breathing regular. If I'm not overinterpreting, he seemed relieved to talk about "them," to respect the images. Well, wouldn't you know that in this boundary-less system, at that moment someone just walked right in the door and said, "Paco, I've got to take you to a dorm meeting." I watched the image shatter right there on his face. His body tensed as he got up, and he put his fist over his heart. As he went toward the door, I told him we'd talk again very soon; he looked as if he wanted to believe me, but wasn't sure he could. As the door closed, for some reason I grabbed the cassette from the recorder and ran after him. All I said was, "You forgot this." He took it and looked at me; I have no idea what was behind those eyes. As he walked away I realized it was I who felt like La Tigressa. Angry. Caged.

I have more to tell about this whole experience with Paco, and what I learned from it, but the hour is late. I must pack for this next trip, and indeed, I promised a shorter letter (so, nobody's perfect.)

In many cosmologies all life comes from the sea. The sea is believed to contain all potentials. I must try to remember that when I hear the thundering of those horses' hooves.

Yours in the arms of Poseidon,
H.

P.S. Adrian has nicknamed me "Merlina."

～～～～～～～～～～～～～～～～～～～～～～～～～～～～～

December 18, 1987

Dear Merlina!

First of all, from the data you gave me, I want to offer my thoughts on your work with Paco.

Re: his connection to the caged feminine, La Tigressa. Even in all her wildness she was the keeper of his heart. Tigers are Mars and Uranus, and his Mars is in Aquarius in the fifth house, the place of the heart.

So, in order to relate to her (with his Moon in Capricorn in the fourth house) Paco had the resourcefulness to cage/restrain her (Moon in Capricorn). Caged or not, at least she would be his. He could stay connected to some feeling. Your question about the zookeeper was wonderful. It permitted Paco to reveal that even with all of the limitation he could still stay related to the feminine, to his soul, via the zookeeper "who had the key." He wasn't afraid of being harmed; he was afraid of losing the connection ("she'll run away") to his soul. Perhaps a caged connection to soul is better than no soul at all. Poor kid, but lucky for him to have worked with you. If the work continues, please keep me posted.

Now I must ask you if you can spare any blessings or incantations. If you're interested in moonlighting, I think I need the services of a white witch.

I am thrilled about your interest in exploring the relationship between dreams and astrology. What I'm finding so far, is that my patients' dreams blend exceedingly well with astrological imagery. This combination provides an exciting spring board into the imaginal dialogues which then usually focus on a prominent dream figure or astrological image.

I have no clinical examples to show you, but I'm working on it. In the meanwhile, here's a recent dream of mine for you to probe:

12/11/87 - The Dream

> *I was alone inside a cave, a very different cave this time. A grey, misty fog invaded the cave's opening. A sense of melancholy pervaded my entire being. I was fearful of being trapped by this moor-like mist, so I stepped outside. The cave was at the edge of a cliff. A dark, moody, turbulent sea waited below. There was no escape. To return to the cave would mean isolation and eventual death. To try and climb down the rocky precipice would probably mean the same. I returned to the cave. I noticed some writing and picture images on the cave's walls. Two men were pictured in a fighting, war-like pose. The writing was obscured and hard to read. I was startled by the sudden appearance of a*

> *withered-looking old man. He was half-dressed in*
> *a wet, tattered toga. I could tell he must have once*
> *been virile, strong, potent. He now looked as if he*
> *had been drained of his physical and emotional*
> *strength. He looked pleadingly into my eyes. I*
> *knew he was the god Poseidon. I wondered, had he*
> *come to save me?*

There you have it. I will detour from dream talk for a moment in order to let you in on some reflective thoughts that I had just prior to the dream. I had some surprise reactions to our telephone conversation.

After we spoke, I found myself growing more and more embarrassed, even ashamed, by what in retrospect seemed like my grandiose, inflated notions of giving voice to an imaginal astrological approach. Who did I think I was, anyway? Waves of imaginal possibility were rapidly becoming waves of depression, doubt, and anxiety. I wondered, why the loss of interest? What had happened to the faithful attitude which I/we had so lovingly held during our telephone conversation? Was this merely an example of what Jungians refer to as "enantiodromia"? Had a psychological state or condition turned into its opposite? I grew more and more befuddled.

I'd barely begun to process this descending state of soul, or to see into and through the dream which preceded it when a waking experience took place to parallel the dream's intensity.

On December 12th I was driving to a family dinner when my legs began to tremble and shake with great violence. It felt as if they had an electrical current running through them. Filled with fear and panic, I drove to a nearby friend's house, where I collapsed in sobs. Terror pervaded my body. My heart raced and pounded unceasingly. When not seized by the electric-like current, my whole body felt as if it were crying. Strange, but that's how it felt. The top of my head threatened to come off with pain and I needed to hold on to my body. My fear was if I didn't hold on, I would leave this earth. It was like some sort of seizure except that I was conscious. After about four hours, the intensity lessened. My legs felt like rubber and what had been my predictable, comfortable body, world, and psyche felt violated and shocked. It was as if I'd been attacked and robbed by an unknown entity and it had stolen from me something which I would never regain. Stunned, I sat sipping tea. You're going to get a laugh out of this. Instead of running to the emergency room, I turned to the ephemeris. Why wouldn't this astrologer turn to the ephemeris in order to make sense of her world, even at a chaotic time like this? Several gods caught my attention. Their movements are worth noting:

Transiting Mars (attack) and Pluto (death) were in Scorpio, within a degree of my second house Sun (the physical body, the lion and the heart.) At the same time, they opposed natal Jupiter (excess of anything) and Saturn (restraint) conjunction. Transiting Saturn (fear) and Uranus (shock) were conjunct my third house cusp (neurological conditions, driving) and squared to natal Neptune (the image king) in the twelfth house (home of archetypes and Jung's collective unconscious).

Are you still standing? My God, what archetypal forces, or powers, or gods had appeared and had been unleashed? That's both a statement and a question.

You don't need to do much sleuthing to see how the dream images mirror the astrological images and how these were personified in my erratic and drastic bodily symptoms. It seems like I've filled our entire correspondence with James Hillman, but his ideas are always of great comfort to me. I went back into one of his earlier works in search of this passage which seemed so pertinent:

> *Because symptoms lead to soul, the cure of symptoms may also cure away soul, get rid of just what is beginning to show, at first tortured and crying for help, comfort, and love but which is the soul in the neurosis trying to make itself heard, trying to impress the stupid and stubborn mind— that impotent mule which insists on going its unchanging obstinate way. The right reaction to a symptom may as well be a welcoming rather than laments and demands for remedies, for the symptom is the first herald of an awakening psyche which will not tolerate any more abuse. Through the symptom the psyche demands attention. Attention means attending to, tending, a certain tender care of, as well as waiting, pausing, listening. It takes a span of time and a tension of patience. Precisely what each symptom needs is time and tender care and attention. Just this same attitude is what the soul needs in order to be felt*

and heard. So it is often little wonder that it takes a breakdown, an actual illness, for someone to report the most extraordinary experiences of, for instance, a new sense of time, of patience and waiting, and in the language of religious experience, of coming to the center, coming to oneself, letting go and coming home.[8]

In light of what I've just recounted to you, the passage speaks for itself.

Here are a few of my thoughts on how astrological imagery is conveyed in the dream. The cave (Saturn) was smothering (Saturn again), antagonistic (Mars), and constraining to the movement of life (Sun, Pluto). The stormy sea (Neptune) threatened death (Pluto.) The cave's walls were etched with figures at war (Mars and Pluto), yet no solution could be found in the words. It was as if psyche had released images but withheld their meaning. My imaginal horse was at a standstill! The dream figure Neptune was in a state of siege, ravaged and in rags, his potency drained, (Saturn conjunct Uranus.) Who was I (as dream ego) kidding? Neptune couldn't save me. *Perhaps he appeared only so that I might save him.*

My body, my psyche, my horoscope all clamored for attention. They were at war, in conflict, stripped of imagination and libido, and death-oriented—or so it seemed.

---

[8] Moore, Thomas, ed., *A Blue Fire: Selected Writings by James Hillman*, Harper & Row, Publishers, New York, NY, 1989, p.18-19

I didn't stay alone that evening, and I called the doctor. I'm in the process of a complete physical. The results will be here in two days. The symptoms have toned down, yet they persist at a chronic low level. I will let you know immediately how things turn out.

Needless to say I've been greatly impacted by the events of the last several days. I feel deeply changed. I was so worried about the figure of Neptune saving me in that dream. Now I see that indeed he had. I'm beginning to know the living experience of your lovely reference to the word "sacred." Something sacred has indeed been touched in spite of my being scared.

In the aftermath of this recent trauma, I've begun a little research into the mythic details of Poseidon. I was intrigued to discover that he was given a colt at his birth by his mother Rhea. I imagine this was preferable to being stashed in the belly of his father Saturn/Chronos.

I also found that Poseidon is often represented mythically as a horse, and that he is attracted to and often appears in reactions to constrained conditions. Perhaps unbridled, imaginal horses do indeed carry psyche's messages. It is Poseidon's job to open things up.

In light of the preceding events, I feel that the dream and my waking reflection prior to the dream both point to my rather superficial involvement with psyche. Sure, I want an imaginal astro-psychotherapeutic approach to materialize, but is my interest in the images superficial? Perhaps I've been riding a safe wooden horse. Poor Neptune had to leave his watery element to get my attention. *I was so concerned with the collective image of adding something of significance to the astro-psychological pot that I neglected to be genuinely concerned and caring for the images themselves.* Were the images fated to drown in the troubled waters of psyche, my psyche?

My presentation was too pat, too constrained, my attitude lacked the sacred respect that an imaginal approach deserves. There was revolt and eruption into chaos. Poseidon and my own bodily reactions saved me from a too personal, too ego-centered approach to the images of psyche, horoscope, and life. That imaginal high horse that I was riding literally threw me. Bodily symptoms echoed the need to let go, to flow freely. I'm O.K. I trust that whatever physical problems I have can be treated.

I'm engaging the dream-figure Neptune in an imaginal dialogue and will send it to you.

This time I intend to find out who he is. I've mounted the horse again, differently this time. Don't worry about me. I'm returning home.

You see, I too am in the arms of Poseidon.

Much love,
J.

December 24, 1987

Dear Judie,

I've resisted calling you to find out about the results of your physical because I've wanted to hold out hope that you indeed had an encounter with the god; and I haven't wanted to dilute that experience—for you or for me—by "chatting" about it. I fear the human tendency to say, "Oh, it's probably just ..." and thus dismiss any further exploration of what might be resonating on a deeper level. So, please know that I'm, of course, concerned, but trust that you'd have let me know if there's a literal alarm being sounded.

Beyond that, let me say that I'm speechless! And impressed. I really think you're on to something here and I'm feeling quite a personal conflict as I type this. As you can see from the date, it's Christmas Eve and I'm quite a jumble of feelings. I'd planned to spend tonight and tomorrow with friends in upstate New York, but about three days ago I found myself in the throes of a hideous virus that the kids are all passing around, AND I have to go down south again on the 26th at the crack of dawn. I'm sitting at the typewriter right now because I'm feeling relatively ambulatory and coherent, but that might change momentarily. Viruses are Plutonian, are they not? Well, Don and Leslie are like family to me—dear, warm, nurturing people—but I'm just too sick to drive down and be with them. This Persephone has been abducted from her Demeterian friends by a virulent manifestation of Pluto in her body and forced into submission. For what purpose I know not.

Persephone was "Kore" (the Greek word for "girl") before she became "she who loves the night" (quite an identity switch.) I suspect that I've been a bit Kore-esque these last weeks—functioning in a role assigned, an identity of sorts, but still pulled hither and yon by concerns in the "upper world" of day. A kind of perpetual case management. Manifested all the more by this flying back and forth so much, moving in and out of vastly different energies, geographies, architectures, personalities. A crisis here, a problem there, trouble over at the main hall. The feeling/image is of being pulled up and out of my rootedness; when I'm set down again, the roots just kind of sprawl out on the ground with no place to be fed and watered, as they must be, in the deep dark.

Right now I'd most like to attend, at length and in depth, to your wonder-full letter. I, too, would like to respect your images (and their amazing astrological correlatives) and comment thought-fully and soul-fully on your power-full experience with the physical manifestations of those images. But here I find myself going, sadly, quite contrary to Hillman's wise counsel that,

> *The right reaction to a symptom may as well be a welcoming rather than laments and demands for remedies, for the symptom is the first herald of an awakening psyche which will not tolerate any more abuse ...*

I *know* he's right and yet see that I resist attending to these symptoms—I want remedies, I "need" to get on that plane Saturday morning without this stuffed head so that I won't writhe in agony when the plane takes 20 minutes to land. This is the aberrant side of Poseidon/Neptune, isn't it? I want a fix, a drug, a medicine that will get me up and out when I know very well that psyche has tolerated too much abuse and needs me to go down and in. The irony of being inattentive to my humanity on the eve where, we are told, even God manifested as a human, does not escape me. Hillman cautions, "It takes a span of time and a tension of patience." "Tension" from the Latin meaning "a stretching," and here I do the opposite and coil up. This virus tells me to surrender, and some arid voice in me says "never." I fear that I am in your cave and am struck by the timeliness of *your* dream in *my* life right now.

I have transiting Saturn in the seventh house, opposite my natal Saturn in the first these days: *constraint holding a mirror to itself.* The image is of me in the middle being pulled in a tug-of-war by both these Saturns, and all the while Hades/Pluto has hold of one ankle. I still struggle with the illusion I can get free of his grasp, but we both know he will abduct me sooner or later. We both know that I must go— that it's only a matter of time, a matter of Saturn.

And what you see in all of this is my failure to respect and engage the images. I know there are consequences for this (your letter is profound confirmation of that) and still I naively hope that I'll be granted a dispensation. What hypocrisy! To give a place to Paco's "Tigressa" and not listen to the weeping (and weeping it is) of my own soul. Is this where the expression "There will be hell to pay" gets a literal interpretation? Mary Renault observed in *The King Must*

Die that "It is never wise to neglect the gods of the place, wherever one may be." I've seen the consequences of that neglect in so many lives and in so many places in the world, as have you. My body tells me too clearly right now to consider those consequences, and I resist that descent so fiercely. Now I must sign off, as I'm truly not feeling well and must at least rest. Thank you so much for your observations about my experience with Paco—I take them with me on this next trip and still have so much to tell you from the last one. You hold, dear friend, the thread as I wander in this self-made labyrinth. I shall be forever grateful.

I hope to have news soon of my participation in what sounds like a lovely gathering of folks—a kind of salon for the soul being formed—here in the north early in the new year. A local therapist told me that a very interesting guy named Tom Moore is putting it together, and she thinks I should meet him. He's also forming an institute to study the imagination, knows Hillman, wants like-minded people to get together and talk about soul. I'm so, so ready. Starving, really.

Blessings and love to you from your beleaguered Merlina

Postscript: December 24, 1987

After signing off with blessings and love on this Christmas Eve, I spent the next two hours tossing and turning and tossing some more, images and a sporadically scribbled intense dialogue with a soul figure moving in and out of my consciousness (I can pass that along to you at another time). I remembered a lecture Charles Poncé gave at the Jung

Institute in L.A. in which he drew out of Jung's thinking and mythological sources the notion that the gods hide in our diseases and that our attention is drawn to them through symptoms or illness, (the same theme of Hillman's that you just shared with me.) Our feelings, our emotions are what liberate—and even feed—these gods, archetypal powers, images.

I thought of the phrase, "I'm not 'feeling' well," and the much-asked question, "How are you feeling?" This is what soul spoke of so sadly to me, letting me know I had, in fact, been doing an altogether poor job of feeling lately, that I had been living my personal life without very much real emotion or tenderness while attending to everyone and everything else. This school has become my alembic.

It was clear that the images of my soul were alive but not well, and were indeed, growing drier by the day. I was offering only a burned up, scorched mirage—a seventh house Sagittarian partnership—with fires of too much vision reaching outward to too many and not at all inward to my solitary self. The soul's voice had every right to complain, and it's time I attend to that in earnest.

H.

December 30, 1987

Dear Hadley,

I tried to call you over Christmas and must have just missed you. I suspected your health had improved by the morning of your departure. I say that because of your stated willingness to encounter and acknowledge that soul-figure. Do you suppose it had found a hiding place in your flu symptoms? Yes, I know according to Freud sometimes a cigar is just a cigar, but what fine smoke screens cigars provide for the muffled pleas of neglected soul-figures! Your caring for soul speaks volumes. Yea! Soul wants what it wants when it wants it. And here is the important piece: you attended to soul's need.

I continue to be touched by your poetic references to those planetary dialogues—the astrological aspects. You referred to transiting Saturn opposite your natal Saturn as "constraint holding a mirror to itself." Then in an earlier letter you made reference to a Saturn-Sun aspect as "time pressing on the heart." If only we astro-psychological people could include in our language the use of word-images, or word-paintings. How rich it would be to say to a client when speaking of a Saturn transit to the Sun: "It must feel rather like time has been pressing on your heart?" You have a real gift with these phrases. I love the way they reflect as well as speak to psyche. Send more.

Now for my medical news. So far my physical work-up has informed myself and my doctor of one irrevocable fact. I have entered the menopause. Gulp. News of this experience had the same kind of impact upon me as the arrival of the menses and the announcement of pregnancy. The difference is that the end of the menstrual cycle, while just as shocking as the onset, has been a much tougher idea for this puella to digest. Move over Persephone: another eternal girl is about to try and claw her way back from hell!

It seems that, in many cases, as one's estrogen dries up—and this goes too long unnoticed—the result for some women is severe panic attacks along with other neurological and metabolic changes. I've already conveyed these to you in great detail. Can you hear my cries? "Pluto don't take me, don't abduct me out of this psychological realm of eternal girlhood which I long ago outgrew, and which I yet fight to hold on to." Indeed I've been robbed of something which I can never regain. I don't mind at all losing the monthly menstrual cycle and child-bearing capabilities. What is so damned hard to face is the ultimate bodily end—old age and death. The shocking way in which the menopause has announced itself to me will not let me forget this certainty: I, like everyone else, am going to die someday. I have my psychological work cut out for me.

Do you recall a while back when we discussed Crane's painting of the horses? I've been living with unexpressed feelings about the subject, and as a result I began an imaginal dialogue with the dream figure Poseidon/Neptune. I'm enclosing it here. Notice how long it took me to be interested in "him." I would love your response to the way the dialogue illuminates and brings the transits around my natal horoscope to life. Responding to the dialogue in this way will give you a good idea of how useful this method can be not only for the individual but for the professional as well.

Belated Happy Birthday and Happy New Year.
Here's to salvation.
Your old Cronee!
J.

An Imaginal Dialogue With Poseidon

J: I want to start off by telling you how pathetic you looked to me in my dream. I want to say "wretched" really, just wretched.

P: I disappointed you....

J: Yes, but I feel terribly guilty about it. You looked at me like a homeless man about to give me his last dollar.

P: What's the matter? You're not worth it?

J: I don't know. What happened to beauty, fantasy? I don't want to be stuck—trapped—in a damp cave with a withered, old, stripped down version of you.

P: What do you want?

J: I want romance on the high seas.

(Here you will notice how I immediately spend several minutes hammering away about what I wanted and deprecating him.)

P: I can't help you with that.

J: I hate you, damn it. You've let me down. My whole body trembles. I feel hot and odd and shaky and sad and scared. Can't you get me out of this?

P: Don't blame me for that. You're not going to use me in your second half of life the way you used me in the first half.

J: I don't get it.

P: Your romanticized notions won't serve you much longer.

J: Romanticized notions about what?

P: About psyche, images, love. Either you go deeper and more fully into these things or you might as well forget it.

J: What do you mean forget it?

P: What I want is real commitment, real service to psyche. If, as you proclaim, I am the "image king," then it's about time you take your own words to heart.

J: You're pompous, you know that?

P: And you're angry because I've called your bluff. Don't you get it? There's a whole world waiting for you.

J: There is? (finally a humble utterance)

P: Yes, do you think I entered your dream cave because I had nothing better to do?

J: Why did you come?

P: I didn't come for your attack. I came to remind you that when you notice me, really notice me, no matter how desolate, isolated or desperate you are, I will connect you to your psychic condition. That's the only salvation I offer.

J: That's what you ask of me?

P: Yes.

J: I can't shake that image of you standing there in that dream ... the pleading in your eyes haunts me. You were so vulnerable, but so unafraid. It was your vulnerability ...

P: Yes, I'm vulnerable, and so are images. Images are terribly vulnerable.

J: I long to be that vulnerable, but I dread it terribly.

P: Ah, you care about me!

P: Well then stop hiding me. I can't eradicate your troubles but your own vulnerability can. If you're reading Hillman, really reading him, then you would know that about me. To stay in touch with images is to stay in touch with your psychic condition. That's my job. To lead you there.

J: I thought I was doing that.

P: Only on the surface.

J: You really did grab my attention when you showed up like that in the cave. Now I feel sad.

P: About what?

J: About how pathetic you needed to become in order for me to take notice. It's I who am pathetic. It's I who feel inferior.

~ ~ ~ ~ ~ ~ ~ ~ ~ ~ ~ ~ ~ ~ ~ ~

At this point our respective lives took over. Judie had to devote all her free time to working on her dissertation, and Hadley was consumed by long hours and intense work at the school's two branches; after a few more months she decided, for many reasons, it was best to resign in order to work as a private practice therapist in town. So the pleasure of this correspondence which meant so much to us was set aside as myriad obligations took center stage.

In 1990 Hadley returned to California and resumed her private practice there. Having completed her dissertation, Judie was well-established in her own office by then. Over the next two decades, the two of us continued to meet, talk, work, attend seminars and conferences, explore the ways in which astrology and psychotherapy could enhance one another. But it was not until Judie found that box of old letters in the spring of 2013 that the idea of expanding our initial discussion and committing to a new kind of "correspondence" occurred to either of us. We'd both become so acclimated to email that it seemed the obvious vehicle. We were pleasantly surprised at the discussion that unfolded during the following email exchange. The ideas that emerged fostered and highlighted both the differences and similarities in our approaches to reimagining astrology.

PART 4

Acorn Sprouting

We're all evolving souls in a meaningful universe....

-- Steven Forrest, *Skymates*

From: Judie
To: Hadley
Subject: A lost treasure

You'll never guess what turned up today while I was cleaning out my office! I found a dusty old cardboard box, and inside was that manuscript I put together from the letters we wrote on reimagining astrology. Do you remember? Doesn't it seem like lifetimes ago? The letters seem to have stopped after the first few months, and I must've filed this material away for future reference. In many ways, it seems more pertinent now than when we originally wrote it. So here's a big question: Would you be interested in refreshing it, resurrecting it, perhaps infusing this mysterious never-to-be-forgotten manuscript with new life? Your thoughts?

From: Hadley
To: Judie
Subject: A lost treasure found

"Never guess" barely says it! My time back east was such a whirlwind, and thinking back on our respective transits and progressions for the three years I was there, I'm surprised we managed to exchange any letters at all—and on typewriters! I can't really think why the correspondence would've ended. I know I got more consumed with layers of issues and problems I had with the school (Saturn & Pluto my constant companions then), so that probably conspired with your Ph.D. work to use up huge chunks of time and energy on both sides.

From: Judie
To: Hadley
Subject: That lost treasure

Well, when it comes to memory these days, I'm far from perfect. What I do know is that we'd written about reimagining astrology post-dissertation. Still, until now it's somehow had a hard time finding its way back into our hearts and souls. But it's reached mine, so I move we resurrect it and bring it back to life. Are you willing?

From: Hadley
To: Judie
Subject: Available for treasure hunt

It's pretty amazing. All I can say is Psyche doesn't play small and now seems to have reached across time to draw us into extending that particular conversation. Years ago I heard Clarissa Pinkola Estés say that all projects have a life of their own, and some have to go into a pot on the back burner to simmer for longer than we could ever imagine. In my own writing experience, I've come to believe a project has its own unique spirit, and said spirit has its own timing, its own agenda. So in response to your suggestion that we refresh and resurrect this one, I say yes, yes, let's do it. Maybe it wants us to know it's time to launch an updated perspective on reimagining astrology out into the world.

After your initial email I was thinking about how your work with images not only spans these many years but has also materialized into your beautiful sculpting work while mine's gone in the direction of writing and poetry.

From: Judie
To: Hadley
Subject: Images work in mysterious ways

I've learned there's no way to fight the images that emerge and ask to be sculpted. They begin as psyche's images but ultimately become embodied in physical form. For me anyway, they're often in complete contrast to what my ego thought it had planned! And they always have much to teach me about where soul is, what *it* wants and what *it* needs. But since our dialogue here is related to our professional lives, I would say obviously the concern and work with images most often appears clinically in sessions with patients.

From: Hadley
To: Judie
Subject: Yes, images work in mysterious ways

So where do you want to pick this up? As we diverge and converge on our respective paths, we don't talk all that much about how we each work. How often do you use imaginal dialogues with clients these days? Images in dreams tell me where I am in my own heart and in the soul of the world. We both pay a lot of attention to dreams, but that's not quite the same thing.

From: Judie
To: Hadley
Subject: Rediscovered treasure leading to many images of soul

Even though I discovered Hillman and other archetypal/-imaginal thinkers in the early eighties, my clinical work is never fully in the imaginal realm, or fully in any realm or method of practice, for that matter. As you know, I'm sure, sometimes it's still just straight ahead short-term crisis work—the problem, the resolution, then basically in and out. But there's always a sprinkling of astrological sessions here and there, some out in the open as part of a psychotherapy session, some not. There's longer term depth work, usually with the extended cases requiring longer treatment, but with that comes the struggle with insurance companies, their rules and regulations involving managed care issues.

Several factors urged me into forging a "more perfect union" of psychological astrology with imaginal psychology. You're familiar with my doctoral dissertation, so you know I added an imaginal astropsychological perspective to the existing body of astrological thought; that's an example of my growing relationship to the imaginal approach and process.

When I was working on the dissertation I also began to encourage patients, as well as astrological clients, to incorporate more of a depth perspective in the work, and one way of doing that was to encourage them to work with imaginal dialogues during our sessions. This coordinated with Hillman's lectures and publications and other written material and lectures by many of the professors at Pacifica Graduate Institute. Sometimes patients would bring in their written dialogues, other times we'd do it on the spot right in my office. Over all those years, the use of imaginal methods just sort of seeped in more and more clinically. A man in the audience once asked Hillman how he could be more like him in his work, and Hillman told him he should "use my soil and grow your own trees." Well, I guess I've been in the process of growing my own trees.

I don't really think it is possible to say just exactly what it was or is that draws someone to one aspect of professional practice over another. Who knows really? Why did I gravitate so strongly to the archetypalists, their predisposition toward myth, images, and soul? Why were you driven (I'm a witness!) to travel for so many years in Greece and immerse yourself in studying the archetypes of Greek myth? Then working to integrate that with family systems theory and evolutionary astrology—exploring past lifetimes as they relate to this one? Both Richard's [Idemon] and Steven's [Forrest] work helping steer your travels on down "Eternity Road," as you call it. Hillman's work offered me the ideal hook on which to hang my imagination. In keeping with the theme of the subject at hand, our choices were not our own, but the call of each of our daimons! Perhaps our soul's codes led us down different roads but on related paths, provoked all the while by a similar purpose.

Aside from Hillman's work being the main impetus behind my dissertation, I was academically required, and also wanted personally, to add something new to the field of astrological psychology. What came to me was the obvious goal of incorporating something new into the dissertation's methodology. Clinical examples using imaginal dialogues not only satisfied academic requirements, but more importantly made a place for soul to speak, to be heard and honored within the kind of archetypal/astrological dialogues that prompt the expression of psyche's images. I've seen emotional blocks loosen and the ultimate release of affect bring greater consciousness to the presenting problem at hand; and, if one is lucky, channels of creativity are unblocked.

From: Hadley
To: Judie
Subject: Imaginal dialogues vs. active imagination

How do *you* differentiate the experience of imaginal dialogues from the process of Jung's active imagination?

From: Judie
To: Hadley
Subject: Imaginal dialogues vs. active imagination

For me, for some reason, imaginal dialogues just seem simpler. My own sense of it is that they're less of a spiritual discipline (i.e., having a process that must be adhered to) than active imagination. Both serve psyche and consciousness in their own way. In imaginal dialogues one works mainly with the image, or images, as they arise. That's the methodology, probably greatly simplified, as I understand it. I could say that it's more like serving the images as opposed to serving Jung's Self. Yet, even that seems too simplistic and goal-focused.

Personally, I'm more comfortable saying that imaginal work has led me to having more spontaneous access to creativity and a greater ease in honoring the images just as they are. There's no particular method as such. The images of soul that arise are primary, and by serving them, caring for and listening to them, they in turn often respond by honoring and assisting me—or us—when we have truly placed our trust and faith in them. In fact you could say I'm bi-imaginal—I like my images, both ways: as ocular literalisms as well as psyche's imaginal paintings!

The point is that astropsychological images of soul are like mini-stories, tiny vignettes that appear to me as meditations as I analyze and perceive a horoscope. They're powerful, rich gifts of psyche, affording life-long themes, or as Hillman has noted, they're bits and pieces of healing fiction,[9] like scenes from a dream, (my words) that act to deepen the interpretation of the archetypal astrological complexes within the analysis of a birth horoscope. In this way, one enters one's own story, with the option of writing it onward.

I've found that the astrological archetypal complexes Rick Tarnas and others speak about seem to blend more easily and effectively with the psychological concerns of patients. When imaginal dialogues become part of the therapeutic process, patients work on them, with them, as a way of discussing a particularly challenging archetypal complex within their horoscope. It's fascinating how this type of work can run absolutely parallel either to a dream or to the presenting problem we've been working on in their therapy. Many patients actually engage in an imaginal dialogue with the imaginal figures and/or gods within an astrological configuration. There's no need in these cases to present an entire horoscope, but if you would like I can provide a sample of the synthesis between the patient's concerns, the chart's archetypal complex in question and the imaginal dialogue she produced at home prior to our session. Let me know. I'll get it to you tomorrow, but I have to be some place now.

---

[9] Hillman, Op. cit.

From: Hadley
To: Judie
Subject: Please do!

When you think about it, we're all born into someone else's story, aren't we? So then, we could say that deeply feeling into how best to write one's own story forward from within one's self, one's essence, is vital—and surely part of our karmic predicament. And, yes, I'd like an example of a synthesis.

From: Judie
To: Hadley
Subject: A necessary Veil

I'm thinking of a client who presented with difficulties expressing feelings—especially in the company of significant others. She was dynamite as the head of a corporation but generally ill at ease and almost phobic in social situations. This acute problem was circumstantially heightened at the time of her initial visit.

I immediately suspected there were challenging issues from the archetypal complex of astrological Hades/Pluto aspects, perhaps at birth, perhaps activated in terms of cycles currently operating in the chart. Since becoming more familiar with Richard Tarnas's superb work, I now link the mythic figure with the planet as an archetypal complex when speaking of either one.

She initially came for quite a few counseling sessions, and after I got to know her a bit better, I asked if I might have a look at her horoscope. She agreed. And it turned out that she was a Virgo with Hades/Pluto closely conjunct her Sun, and both are placed in the social, partnership, marital 7th house. Added to that is the formation of a challenging ninety-degree relationship to her Moon in Sagittarius in the 10th house of parent, career, status, worldly goals, etc. With all that flexible, planetary mutability, one would think she'd have more access to sharing via verbal expression. But instead of boosting my client's social life and interaction, her Sadge Moon focuses—lavishes—its excesses on discussion and ideas related to her career goals and achievements (10th house) rather than her intimate partnerships (7th house).

Long story short, her Sun in Virgo struggles under the dominion of Hades/Pluto in the social 7th house, the area concerned with establishing more personal partnerships. This dynamic appears to have eclipsed her self-confidence socially, resulting in a kind of freezing of her ability to access verbal expression. She's desirous of one-on-one intimacy but she uses that energy to run a high-powered company while her intimate expressions with others are virtually non-existent.

During our astrological exploration, I asked if she could tell me what it was like to have felt this social discomfort for most of her entire life. That question hit her hard. At first she defended against this discussion by deflecting my question. She effusively evaded by describing her career-laden 10th house professional life, the responsibilities, long hours, and stress-inducing demands. There was just that one question from me, and before we knew it we were in an imaginal dialogue together!

JH: Can you give me an image of what this unrelenting struggle must be like for you?

C: [defensively] What? I have no photos here. You mean…

JH: Not a photo.

C: What then?

JH: I mean an image. A picture, but a word picture.

She became tearful, appeared uncomfortable, looked confused. I stayed quiet, then heard a meek utterance of one word.

C: Veil

JH: Veil? What kind of veil?

Obviously, just her utterance of that term, which appeared to surprise her, had provoked some intense feeling. Tears came. I didn't overly soothe or reward her expression of what clearly were real tears. I quietly noted the similarity between the words "vale" as in a vale of tears and "veil" in order to clarify which one was correct. I was silently encouraged by the reference to the image of a veil, and I wondered if a psychological experience like Hillman's "seeing through" might be in the offing? I also wondered if somewhere in her the image of a marriage veil might be lingering.

JH: Yes, go on.

C: [sobbing quietly] It's so heavy, so heavy. How can a veil be heavy?

JH: Perhaps you've worn—carried it—a long time .

C: But it's transparent.

JH: You're doing fine.

I hung back from any more interpretation. There was a long silence here.

C: It's protection. But it's invisible.

Hades/Pluto, the god of invisibility, had entered with the term *invisible*. I felt encouraged.

JH: Does this veil have a color?
C: Yes. It's nude, flesh-colored.
JH: And the fabric?
C: It's barely there, but...

She giggled through the tears.

JH: What's the laughter about?
C: The term "barely there" as in the underwear brand....

I smiled, avoiding the many responses that might sidetrack the dialogue and defend the emerging feelings. Then came a kind of realization...

C: It imprisons and comforts me all at the same time. It's always with me.

JH: Always? How long in years?

As she spoke she seemed to regress in her presentation, moving backwards through time from her chronological age of forty-two to about age fifteen.

C: As far back as I can recall...my teens.

JH: Yes.
C: I'll miss its invisible protection.

From that statement I suspected that our work was beginning to take a turn. Was she ready to emotionally risk letting go of the invisible protection by which she'd become imprisoned?

My suspicions were definitely confirmed. *Invisibility, a crucial aspect of the archetypal complex of astrological Hades/Pluto, had at last entered the picture and been named.*

JH: Can you remove the veil here, now—just for a little while?
C: No, well, not exactly. What I mean is I don't know. I don't know.

She grew quiet. Tears began to flow profusely. To me, her tears indicated that she was acknowledging at least the possibility of letting go of this defensive protection.

JH: The ability to *see through* something—such as the veil— to what is essential can also be an asset.
C: You mean like it's, I mean, my...

There was a long pause. She wasn't finding the right words. I waited but decided to supply the word for her. She'd worked hard!

JH: Protection?
C: Yes, my *invisible* protection.

JH: It doesn't have to keep everyone away. Perhaps it can help you discern who to let in. Invisibility may end up being its positive value.

With attention to the veil, that one image just as it appeared, we began to get someplace. We didn't define, research, quote anyone, excessively interpret, or overly characterize. We honored the image just as it came through. The astrological Hades/Pluto (the invisible) was the carrier of the image of that veil. Our attention, our interest, remained on that veil. Later we were able to get into the other astrological aspects, planetary placements, family dynamics, and other related psychological reasons she needed that invisible piece of clothing. *But we did not start there.* As it turned out, eventually the metaphorical image of that veil became a symbol full of meaningful, detailed, psychodynamic information. We allowed the image to tell us what it was and what it needed. Like explorers and fellow travelers joined together in a pursuit, we explored this veil, this image of soul, together.

Of course, as a professional, I was there to help guide the ship. And yes, I'd evaluated her astrological chart before talking with her about it in order to know how to help guide her effectively. But it was this one archetypal complex, that of the Virgo Sun-Pluto conjunction placed in her 7th house (the symbolic region of the "other")—and its challenging relationship to the lunar light of the Sagittarius Moon in her 10th house (of career, parent, and place in the world)—that linked up so beautifully with her presenting psychological problem.

It was *invisibility*, that initial image of soul associated with the myth of Hades, that opened the door for the astropsychological process that guided us in the direction where we eventually were meant to go.

What about you? Was there a time when the imaginal realm made its presence known to you in a therapeutic context? Or, in any other context for that matter? You rarely refer to these kinds of encounters.

From: Hadley
To: Judie
Subject: The Gypsy in my office

Most definitely—a session I'll never forget! In my first year of private practice, I was about thirty minutes into a standard intake with a new client when "The Gypsy" appeared over my left shoulder.

The client was impeccably dressed in a steel grey business suit, a tailored off-white silk blouse, and black designer stilettos; she sat primly at the edge of the couch, with her expensive handbag and briefcase leaning against it. As I gathered information about her background, it became obvious she'd lived a life wherein asking for help was anathema. I could see she was trying to control her anxiety, and that presenting herself in a therapy office bordered on shameful. That wasn't unusual for a wide swath of the client population, and during my internship I'd found myself quite able to help new clients relax.

On this late afternoon, however, I had no idea what to do with what was unmistakably "present" in the room. I'd never had such an experience before, and it was so sudden and so distracting I could barely look at the client or string words together coherently.

Just behind me to my left was the archetypal (at the time I would've said "cliché") image—presence!—of a six-foot tall gypsy woman, complete with a cascade of long black hair, an off-the-shoulder peasant blouse, tiered bright red skirt pulled seductively up toward her right hip, a tambourine in her left hand, and—oh yes—a red rose between her teeth.

I made every attempt to dismiss whatever this was; I focused intensely on the client and for a moment The Gypsy vanished. Barely a minute later she was back—fiercely—and I finally said to the client: "I'm so sorry. I know I've been recommended to you, but you don't know me, and what I'm about to tell you will make me sound crazy. I assure you I'm not. I don't know what to do with this, but, if I don't tell you what's going on, I won't be able to focus on the rest of this session, and I very much want to do that."

I then described exactly what/who was invisibly hanging out over my shoulder. The client looked startled, as if shaken from sleep, and burst into tears a moment later. "Oh my god! Oh my god! That's *me*! That's who I *really* am! Look at me— look at this suit, these shoes, this 'thing' I've become! I *hate* my life—I want a different one."

On that day I began to learn one of the ways images of soul can present themselves—and how important it is to respect them, not dismiss them. Experiences like that didn't then immediately become common to me, but I did learn that when an image moved across my psychic viewfinder, I'd best attend to it no matter how odd or baffling or out of context it was.

From: Judie
To: Hadley
Subject: That soulful Gypsy

I love the psychic viewfinder metaphor! Striking and beautifully, beautifully stated! There's an old song entitled "The Gypsy in My Soul." You saw the gypsy in her soul and could somehow honor and respect it—the psychological work just had to be about freeing that image of soul in her life. And the courage it took to reveal that image to her. Wow, I'm impressed. Lucky she found you! Did you have her horoscope at the time? If so, did you see the gypsy in her soul there? I'm imagining the two freedom-loving archetypes Jupiter and Uranus were somewhere somehow just dying to get out! Your work with her must've gained new momentum from then on. Can't resist this question: in terms of countertransference, do you remember where The Gypsy in *your* soul was at that time!?

From: Hadley
To: Judie
Subject: That soulful Gypsy

I remember that song very well, though *this* Gypsy woman felt—"looked"—more like the Waylon Jennings or Santana version! Jupiter-Uranus is likely, but no, I had no chart for the client. This was back before computers, and when I did a therapy intake, I got a birth date and whatever other data I could, then waited to see if the client would be receptive to astrological work. Most important to me in this case is that the image brought us together on an entirely different level than would've seemed "predictable" in those first thirty minutes. And, for me, that was the beginning of trusting when an image "enters the room." I've often mused about the word "imagination"—parse it, and it contains instruction: image-in. Let the image in! It comes from a realm beyond knowledge.

Though images don't present themselves as regularly for me as I think they do for you, I've discovered an intriguing way to open the gate so they can come in more often. I've been integrating Lauren Schneider's Tarotpy® system[10] into my sessions. This involves using images from many different sources to "lay the psyche out on the table" with a therapy client. More and more I see that doing this, working this way, enables people to say things that are true, things they just couldn't say—or maybe even access—otherwise. And when I'm working with a chart, sometimes I actually put these

---

[10] Lauren Schneider: http://www.dreamsandtarot.com/tarotpy.htm

images into the chart wheel and show the client. This really brings it alive; it's a fascinating way of deepening my own and my clients' processes. I'll tell you more about it later if you're interested. In any case, I've certainly learned never to ignore an image whenever and however it appears. That's in both my therapy and my astrological sessions as well as when the two are combined.

As for my countertransference at the time of that early, initiating experience, I truly don't remember; but I'm a card-carrying Sagittarius, so I entered this life with a thoroughly en-souled Gypsy.

Say some more about having an ongoing relationship with the images.

From: Judie
To: Hadley
Subject: When an image enters the room

At first it seemed strange to me, but as I became increasingly more comfortable, I noticed that the dialogue with the images seemed to make them more real, more embodied. I developed what I would characterize as an odd, but embodied caring for them. I realized more and more that they're not here just to serve us, to answer our questions, or to solve our problems. What happens for me is that when I'm in an imaginal dialogue with them, I make certain to keep a steady care and concern for them. I often imagine that Robert Bosnak's embodied dream work must have a similar sensation and texture to it in that one feels as if there's an entrance into another realm, invisible yet embodied and real. Don't know if I'm making myself clear....

From: Hadley
To: Judie
Subject: **When an image enters the room**

Quite clear—not least because my own therapist is trained in Bosnak's embodied dream work. It took some getting used to in the beginning, but having it combined with a multi-leveled exploration of the archetypes that show up in my dreams has really enriched my personal work and certainly enhances my ability to help my clients on many levels.

Do you remember that terrific weekend seminar Hillman did at Pacifica in 2007 on "The Art, Practice, & Philosophy of Psychotherapy"? I cherish what he said about psychology being "a discipline of *value*," a way to restore value to the soul as well as to what the soul values. He linked that with the importance of understanding how to use the word "archetypal." He emphasized that using that word "gives big value to what's happening. It's a *value* word—*not* a metaphysical word in the sense of referring to archetypes who are 'up there.' It refers to values that are emotive, recurrent, irrepressible, fundamental, trans-human, ubiquitous— recurring everywhere. In other words, when you say something is 'archetypal,' you're valuing it largely."[11] I think that's so important. Bringing the images into our work more and more lets them know we value them largely; and given

---

[11] Hillman, James. "The Art, Practice, and Philosophy of Psychotherapy." Pacifica Graduate Institute, Carpinteria, CA. June 29-July 1, 2007. Seminar.

what's happening with much of "modern" psychology, surely that's a good thing.

Also, I recently listened back to a talk Bosnak gave at a conference in 1992, and I hear parts of it from a different perspective now. He talked about how each image has its own *necessity* and that *that's* what you have to get to. This called up for me the image of Anangke, the Goddess of Necessity, Mother of the Fates, and a lot of writing I did about her years ago.

From: Judie
To: Hadley
Subject: Where is Evolutionary Astrology in all this?

I do remember that Hillman weekend; it's always good to be reminded of his superb ability to delve back into things we think we know. How wonderful that you've got a firsthand acquaintance with Bosnak's excellent and very avant garde work! I also love that concept of an image having its own necessity. Speaking of necessity and fate, I'm also curious about the many times you went to Greece—it seemed for years like you couldn't *not* go as often as possible! You got totally immersed in the mythology and imagery there, so how did that get integrated—evolve?!—into your work with Evolutionary Astrology? How is one to understand it? I'm wondering how it might differ—or not—from my own approach to a birthchart.

From: Hadley
To: Judie
Subject: Where is Evolutionary Astrology in all this?

From my earliest studies I was continually amazed at how sophisticated various mythologies are when seen as psychological systems, models. Greek culture reached up and grabbed my ankles from the first moment I set foot on the tarmac in Athens, so *that* mythology captured my heart and my imagination most profoundly (though I do believe I was resonating with prior lifetimes spent there). Also, though I don't know why, the Greek names for the planets/gods/archetypes we work with in astrology spoke to my soul more deeply than the Roman names we all learned. In addition, when I asked my Greek teacher how to say "Follow your bliss" in this language I grew to love so quickly, he said the Greeks have no word for personal "bliss." So, for the closest translation in that language, you have to say "Follow your inner divinity"—your daimon. How fitting!

And, since my earliest therapeutic training was in the application of systems theory to human relationships (that was considered revolutionary back in the day!), the concept of the horoscope as a map of our own psychic ecosystem, simply made sense. That that personal ecosystem was ineluctably connected to an ever-expanding number of other systems and thus ultimately connected to the cosmos itself was, to me, irrefutable. Fractals!

All those archetypal figures in the Greek pantheon surrounded and infused the ancient Greeks, animated them, were basic to their lives. So all the stories (and let's remember there are many, many versions) of these figures' interactions yielded rich imagery for me. All the tales—about the conflicts, romances, betrayals, triumphs, separations, reunions, etc., in that gigantic dysfunctional "family" system—are replicated inside us and in every human system repeatedly across millennia. Early history and literature classes—especially Shakespeare!—had taught me that.

But what had always been missing for me was any answer to "*Why* that replication?" I was raised Catholic, with all the horror of a central admonition: "You get this one life, and that's it. Do it right, and you'll go to heaven. Blow it, and you go to hell for all eternity." That never made sense to me—i.e., an "all-loving" god figure being so pathologically rigid—but until I learned about reincarnation and then discovered astrology in my early twenties, I had to just sit with the why. In those early days, too, I still found a lot of reincarnation "lore" either pretty iffy or much too pat (How many Queen Nefertitis could there have been?); and sundry astrological musings about discerning past lives through the birthchart never quite took hold for me. Yet, humanity is full of resurrection stories—including the one central to my childhood faith—so why wouldn't these be metaphors for reincarnation?

Then in the late nineties two things coincided. Hillman's *The Soul's Code* was published—I devoured it; and a therapy client described a completely anomalous emotional breakdown she'd had the previous weekend. I'll omit the details here, but I'd worked with her for over two years, she'd been very forthcoming about her history and worked conscientiously in therapy. By the time the session was over we both believed that her extreme overreaction to a scene (images!) in a very popular film couldn't be traced to anything in her history or current situation. As I sat with her I was overwhelmed with the feeling that something had triggered a traumatic memory from another lifetime—I've coined the term "PL-PTSD" (Past-life Post-Traumatic Stress Disorder)—that something was left unresolved. I remember looking at her chart after the session, but I had no clear method at the time for garnering information that would help her/us.

Around this time my old friend Steven Forrest was really developing his thinking around what would eventually turn into Evolutionary Astrology. It became the missing piece of the puzzle for me—enabling me to pull together the archetypal dynamics of the individual soul unfolding and developing via multiple systems over lifetimes.

From: Judie
To: Hadley
Subject: Evolutionary Astrology & Soul's Code?

I find myself trembling at the vastness of those ideas and their infinite convergence. Wow! And the term PL-PTSD. Love it. So, am I correct in assuming you find a resonance between Evolutionary Astrology and Hillman's *Soul's Code*?

From: Hadley
To: Judie
Subject: EA & SC?

I can't imagine a more perfect explication of Evolutionary Astrology than Hillman's "acorn theory" in that book! In a talk back in 1976 Dane Rudhyar said, "Your chart is the acorn of the oak you can become," but that seemed simply a lovely metaphor until Hillman's breakthrough theory. I could cite paragraph after paragraph—page after page!—but even though he had me at the first sentence—"There is more in a human life than our theories of it allow"—he really had me on page 8:

> *The soul of each of us is given a unique daimon before we are born, and it has selected an image or pattern that we live on earth. This soul-companion, the daimon, guides us here; in the process of arrival, however, we forget all that took place and believe we come empty into this world. The daimon remembers what is in your image and belongs to your pattern, and therefore your daimon is the carrier of your destiny.*[12]

Four pages later he notes: "And this form, this idea, this image does not tolerate too much straying"!

Contemporary psychotherapy puts considerable weight on early childhood experiences—all well and good—but

---

[12] Hillman, James, *The Soul's Code: In Search of Character and Calling,* Random House, New York, 1996, p. 8

Evolutionary Astrology posits that we're also *older* than this body we're inhabiting. EA isn't separate from other approaches, but those of us who use Steven's version of its philosophy in our exploration of a chart accept a number of principles as intrinsic. For example:

- That this is one of many lifetimes for the soul, that there is some pre-existing, meaningful "nature" that comes into this life with us at birth. I've chosen to call it "our cosmic DNA": Divine Natal Agenda. In Hillman's terms: the acorn, yes?

- That the birthchart reflects the soul's evolutionary conditions at birth as well as its intentions to integrate and/or move beyond those conditions—i.e., evolve.

- That the symbols/images in the chart are multi-dimensional and come into expression materially and psychologically according to the individual's level of awareness and the decisions that arise from that awareness.

- That the soul's present life circumstances are an amalgam of necessity and intention—what we've committed ourselves to do in order to evolve into a more conscious be-ing (fulfill the daimon's mission?). Still, we can always—always—choose not to do any number of things—nothing carved in stone here.

From: Judie
To: Hadley
Subject: EA & SC?

So, what happens when Evolutionary Astrology meets depth astrology no matter the preferred inclination? Do they blend, or are they antagonistic? How does one differentiate an evolutionary astrological approach from an imaginal and/or in-depth approach?

From: Hadley
To: Judie
Subject: EA & SC?

I think the *approach* may be somewhat different, but my experience tells me they enhance one another. As you know, we can read the symbols in a chart on *so* many different levels—no symbol ever shows up in exactly the same way for any two people. These are vast archetypal fields we're dealing with. And that constantly presents us with the reality you know so well: that psyche is limitless—unfathomable, really. So, to me, reincarnation can't be described in any concrete terms—no algorithm here, only poetry. I'm a traveler, and hearing The Moody Blues song "Eternity Road" a very long time ago engaged something in my psyche. To me, it seemed to be the perfect articulation—image!—that we're all on an infinite journey, we're traveling Eternity Road. And I named my website to honor that complex phenomenon. When you're traveling, there are all sorts of things to keep in mind, adjustments you must make, things you learn about yourself on each trip. As Jung said, "Life is a luminous pause between two mysteries," and, to me, *that's* the most profound, overriding image. No matter what we say here, there is still this enormous mystery which we can, at best, address only in microcosm.

EA assumes—or imagines!—the birth chart to be partially a result of actions, decisions, mishaps, situations, skipped steps, dilemmas, talents and skills developed, lessons learned, etc., in prior incarnations. It assumes that there are "rememberings" in the emotional body more robust than logic. So, as we evolve and mature over lifetimes, we do so with more complexity, diversity, nuance—with more ability to embrace paradox. And if we were to be both metaphysically and ecologically pragmatic, we might imagine that consciously evolving out of our old patterns in this lifetime would enable us to leave the planet in better shape for our soul's subsequent return! Just a thought.

From: Judie
To: Hadley
Subject: EA & SC?

This thought may be a little far a field from the precision of the topic but, Hadley, you got me jumpin' here! Given all that you've just written in your last few emails, I can't help wondering if we don't get another chance in subsequent lifetimes to correct, re-do, re-experience the things and people that have slipped away through death and out of our lives. Given clients (especially the strictly astrological ones) that know of your approach, I can't help wondering if they'd be chomping at the bit for you to offer pieces of hopeful corrections—hope that past experiences might be, if not healed or regained, then, at the very least, understood in present time. If the client is comfortable with your doing so, how do you, or do you, integrate the past life material into the consultation?

From: Hadley
To: Judie
Subject: EA & SC?

First of all, as we've said earlier, discerning when any of this work is appropriate and for whom is absolutely essential. Secondly, in any astrological consultation—or whenever I may be invited to bring this material into a therapy session— my *primary* focus is what's in the birth chart for this present life. In Hillman's terms, how might this particular acorn become the very best version of its own unique oak tree? Also, not every chart shows a prominent link to the karmic past— i.e., something that says, "This will get in your way to the degree that you stay unconscious of it."

And even with the concept of reincarnation in the room, the purpose of using the birthchart in any kind of session is to have it be of service in the client's life *this* time around! I always inquire as to how the client feels about reincarnation before going forward.

Then, when it's possible to explore this in a session, I offer stories that, according to the chart, could be imagined from the karmic past in order to address what the soul is attempting to do in this lifetime. Those stories are not presented as factual, but they contain images, metaphors, themes (perhaps from myths or fairy tales or periods in history) that somehow resonate with the client, are somehow "true" on a soulful level.

From: Judie
To: Hadley
Subject: EA & SC?

I'm revved up from this exchange and dying for examples! For example?

From: Hadley
To: Judie
Subject: EA & SC?

I have in mind a chart with certain configurations that could call up the image of this soul in the karmic past standing, say, outside the Vatican with the 16th century equivalent of a megaphone and railing passionately against the pope. People listened to her (let's give her that temporary gender assignment); she had a reputation, and people were drawn to her as a symbol of something meaningful to them. This was a person using her voice to challenge a dominant paradigm of that time—a troublemaker, someone taking a stand against the entire logic of the culture on behalf of some truth she felt needed to be told.

Surely this took courage, but the current-life astrological configurations suggest there was an element of foolhardiness, self-righteousness, bravado to her actions as well. So, while it was important at the time that she take a stand, and she had the power of words as a natural talent, her fierce convictions blinded her to the complex motivations, the level of treachery—and likely betrayal by family and/or a lover—around her. The repercussions were probably quite shocking and dire, to the point of the ultimate sacrifice, because the powers-that-be needed to show others the consequences of taking up any similar cause. By silencing her they sought to silence her ideas. It's a familiar story down through millennia—and, again, this isn't necessarily a *true* story, but it's an *accurate* one for this chart.

Her evolutionary future now, in this lifetime, involves finding pockets of peace, love, good and true things to live for; the cultivation of a rich inner life and creative self-expression whether or not anyone else sees it. The trauma-drama on the world stage will be seductive to the ego and still of great interest to her; but for the sake of her soul's evolution her acorn seeks to have her cultivate and maintain perspective, detach, not view the perpetual mess of the world through the old karmic lens. She's learning to find love even in the darkest hour, to notice acts of kindness amidst the horrors—out in the world and inside herself. She's learning to trust again, learning to use the familiar power of words in a much more vulnerable and self-expressive, warm way that could actually move hearts, help people. It's a surprisingly tall order for this soul, but it's encoded in her acorn, she knows it and is working steadily to keep the evolutionary tasks in focus.

From: Judie
To: Hadley
Subject: EA & SC?

More than interesting. Utterly fascinating! I cannot help but be more than a little curious about the signatures of her soul's code represented in and by the archetypal complexes inherent in her chart this time around. Let's have lunch soon and please do bring along some charts so that I can have a look at the archetypal configurations that have led you to these dramatic conclusions. I suspect that your work with anyone having this ... how to say it, "complex fate," would be to guide her toward finding those ways that, as you say, steer her *away* from looking at the world through that "old karmic lens." Any less dramatic examples?

From: Hadley
To: Judie
Subject: EA & SC?

"Less dramatic" may be relative, but let's consider another chart wherein a story with Cinderella-like images unfolds. The chart I'm looking at suggests this person has come in with substantial issues from the karmic past around fairness, a feeling of powerlessness around the ability to assert herself and use her will in a personally effective or, for her, courageous way.

She seems to have entered this life with a considerable amount of karmic stress—and perhaps anger—from feeling like she should, but never could, be in command of her life.

In the karmic past we can imagine she was in some ongoing subservient situation (the Cinderella image) where the psyche was often faced with weighing the "better than/less than" hierarchy in relationships, where there was a great longing for the "I-Thou" experience of mirroring by the parent and/or the other. But the message was that feelings were dangerous; so there may have been a lot of sex as a way of trying to access feelings (and even as a way of surviving) in the karmic past, but not a lot of tenderness and actual connection.

Her soul longed to incorporate a deep experience of the Aphrodite archetype into her life, but it seemed perpetually out of reach. In other words, Eros wasn't accessible in a straightforward way. She had to "be nice," go along to get along, couldn't be prettier or smarter than, perhaps, the mother or some other major female figure[s] in her life, a figure who was also unwilling or unable to defend her regarding issues with the father. So, an absence of safety and feelings of self-doubt seem to have regularly placed her in competition for love, friends, resources, status, and there was an overriding feeling that things just weren't fair. Bereavement, abandonment, betrayal led to an understandable emotional armoring and self-containment— and possibly a defaulting in the early years of this lifetime to partners who mirrored those qualities instead of the ones she was longing for.

In the karmic past this seems to have had its basis in her family but may also have manifested in a broader context where perhaps she had skills and abilities that were never recognized or allowed expression because she was mentored by or subservient or apprenticed to a more powerful figure and couldn't imagine herself as an equal. (I'm picturing Camille Claudel in relationship to Rodin; she was fully as talented and intelligent as he, but to this day she's seldom mentioned without his name entering the attributions.)

Is anything in this story and the images it conjures unusual? No. Great works of art have been written around just such archetypal themes. And as I said in the previous example, this isn't necessarily a *true* story, but it's an *accurately imagined* one for this chart. To the extent the client resonates with it, then we look at what her daimon would have her do this time around.

This soul comes into this lifetime with the wisdom and talents and patterns gleaned from these experiences. In the early years there was a seductive—perhaps unavoidable—"pull" to relive the familiar, painful family and relationship patterns. Yet overall this time around she seems quite determined to be recognized for herself, to have authority and visibility, to wrestle with old issues around vulnerability, worthiness, insecurity and lay claim to a measure of personal power and effectiveness in the world. Her acorn has also set her these tasks to help her discover and evolve into what it means to be in equal-to-equal relationships as well as to experience her Aphrodite-ness in a creative and, ideally, spiritual context. From my perspective, and despite moments of considerable, observable self-doubt, I see her making steady—at times remarkable—progress.

From: Judie
To: Hadley
Subject: EA & SC?

In some ways, if one views the horoscope as a symbol of the daimon's intent, then it's also a map of the soul's intent for this lifetime as viewed through the lens of Evolutionary Astrology. So, do you look at one life at a time or assume some sequence? When you're looking at the chart, is the guiding daimon—who's in charge of our becoming—kind of prompting our life tasks in an interdependent relationship with the next, or past lifetime? Are you saying you perceive unfinished or incomplete life lessons in a horoscope? If so, then the evolutionary astrologer should be able to recognize and point out these resistant, yet necessary patterns to the client?

From: Hadley
To: Judie
Subject: EA & SC?

EA would posit that the daimon's intent comes *from* somewhere—as well as having an intention to *go* somewhere. We aren't looking at life after life sequentially—that just wouldn't be possible, and, in my opinion, it's a useless intellectual exercise. It's not about names and faces and where one's previous bodies were buried. Instead, EA attempts to ascertain what might currently be in the emotional body that's left over from one or more prior incarnations regardless of the sequence in which they were lived. Again, no facts, but an evaluation of what's indicated in many charts: varying degrees of PL-PTSD as well as beliefs, talents, skills, abilities that are brought forward.

From: Judie
To: Hadley
Subject: EA & SC?

I like that phrase "emotional body." I can look back into the first years of my own childhood and find many hints, clues, interests, behaviors that have been there right from my earliest memories. The patterns in my horoscope reflect those and also reflect how they've unfolded during the course of my life. Now I find myself asking if qualities, behaviors, and inclinations carry forward from the last or another lifetime.

From: Hadley
To: Judie
Subject: EA & SC?

I can relate. There are parts of my own chart that have conjured such stark images from the karmic past that I simply must keep them in consciousness in order to honor what I believe my soul wants of me this time around. There are chart indicators that show where we're likely to get stuck in the unfinished business from the past if we don't make it conscious and understand the pull it has on us—familiar default themes and perceptions that are too easily repeated and keep the acorn from growing into a beautiful, fully recognizable oak tree. Believe me, I'm all too familiar with the difficulty of stretching away from my own default issues—it's not that easy! (I'm actually comforted by having learned that an oak tree can take nearly 60 years to mature and produce its first full crop of fruit, that the development of the tree can even include a period of rapid growth for about 80-120 years, followed by a gradual slowing down. Let's keep this in mind, old friend.)

But some people *aren't* carrying a heavy imprint from the karmic past, and the chart shows that, too. Yet EA assumes something generated the chart each of us is born with—i.e., there's a reason we have it—and as Steven points out, *if* there's a reason, that reason *must* exist before we were born. So, what might the story/images around that be? In Hillman's terms I'd phrase that as "Why do we have the particular 'acorn' that we have?" Who knows how many answers there are to that question?!

You work very directly with the images that present themselves to you in the horoscope. When you offer the client an image evoked from your contemplation of the chart, does s/he always or immediately resonate with that image? If not, how do you proceed? If so, where does that image then take you? How do you contextualize it? How does it guide you forward in your work?

From: Judie
To: Hadley
Subject: Offerings

I don't always do the "offering" of an image. Often the client comes up with the name. It varies. Occasionally I'll explain the meaning of a particular archetypal complex and the name of an image of soul that can be used in a dialogue will come directly from that or from a dream.

For example: I had a patient, an unmarried Eastern European man, age 57, whom I'll call "Frederich." He came to me for psychotherapy, and not until we'd been working for approximately six months did the subject of archetypal astrology even arise. This occurred accidently while he was at a dinner party and one of the guests mentioned my name in conjunction with astrology. He tucked that away until the next time we met, at which time he asked if I'd consider having a look at his chart. He wanted to see if it might illuminate what, by this time, was his recalcitrant problem. After several months of frustration he and I had started calling this never-ending source of irritation "The Haunting."

Frederich had lived in the US since he was twenty-four. He came here to be part of a major classical orchestra. When he was a small boy he lived in Europe with his father and paternal grandmother. His own mother had abandoned the family when Frederich was seven; he never saw her again. His father remarried, and he had a younger half-sister. Two years after arriving in the US, Frederich met a young violinist with whom he fell in love. Things had seemed to be going well with her until one day she, too, completely disappeared, without a trace—never to be seen again. He brought a photo of her to one of our sessions along with the last photo he had of his mother before she left. The resemblance between the two women was striking.

Though he was in his mid-fifties when we met, he'd been looking for his mother—and later his young lover—in every nook and cranny of his life since he was seven. I'd looked at his birth information on my own to see if I could make any sense out of what was distressing him. Though the birth time was unavailable, and all I had to go on were the geometrical relationships between the major planetary bodies (a.k.a. archetypal complexes), it was astounding how resonant these were with Frederich's "haunting." It was a relief to finally be able to talk about this troubling heartbreak more openly.

There's one dialogue that I happen to have kept in his astrological file. Patients usually want to keep them— or *forget* to mail them back to me after they've left. Here's the archetypal setup:

1.) His Moon (mother, lover, wife) was located in the sign of Pisces, related to Poseidon/Neptune (archetype of fantasy, idealization imagination, symbolic location of Jung's archetypes).
2.) His Sun was in the sign of Hades/Scorpio and trine the Moon in Pisces.
3.) The archetypal complex of Poseidon/Neptune, god of the watery underworld, archetypal realm and place of images and dreams, was also in the sign of Scorpio.
4.) The lover Aphrodite/Venus was located in the wandering, fiery, don't-tie-me-down sign of Sagittarius.

So, within his horoscope, the underworld realm of Hades/Pluto meets the watery, unfathomable depths of Poseidon/Neptune in a 120 degree aspect—a trine. Normally this trine relationship would facilitate ease of relationship between planetary configurations. However, it's my guess that in his case it functioned like a closed circuit that kept reinforcing his ever-present feelings of loss and the hopeful, endless search to be reunited with an idealized mother/lover. And were he not witness to their symbolically amalgamated flesh-and-blood existence, one would swear he'd imagined both his departed mother and errant lover from the start. He's been haunted by these missing women his whole life, hence *The Haunting!*

Imaginal Dialogue between Frederich and The Haunting

Frederich: I'll start with hate. Yes, that's correct I said hate

The Haunting: (no response)

Frederich: OK…go ahead, disappear. I'm used to that from you.

The Haunting: You're off the wall, out of tune, and soon out of time.

Frederich: I feel cursed by you. Now you've taken to threatening me with loss of life.

The Haunting: No threat. Just a biological fact.

Frederich: Well guess what. I've added something new to my musical repertoire.

The Haunting: (no response)

Frederich: OK…play hide and seek again. I don't care anymore.

The Haunting: Good. Good. Good! (tauntingly)

Frederich: I'm returning to Europe. I've made up my mind.

The Haunting: Fess up. Isn't it really to look for me one last time?

Frederich: NO! I've been offered a job at the conservatory and I'm going to take it. I'm going home. I ran away a long time ago.

The Haunting: (again no response)

Frederich: I should have gone before now....

Frederich told me later that he'd had no conscious idea of taking the position in Europe! He'd received a letter inviting him and had left it on his desk for several weeks. It wasn't until this dialogue that the notion to return emerged into consciousness.

This was a very recent development, and I noticed the archetypal complex of Chronos/Saturn had reached exact transit on his Scorpio Sun at the time this dialogue was written. The archetype of Chronos /Saturn had cleared the way for the past (Saturn) to become an embodied, concrete, real, part of the present. I have a feeling there will be some kind of resolution for Frederich, and he's agreed to stay in touch.

So, now to another question. Hadley, please tell me. How is it—or is it—different to imagine the trajectory of a life being driven by EA concepts vs. a life in which one's daimon facilitates the life trajectory—the daimon as discussed in *The Soul's Code*?

From: Hadley
To: Judie
Subject: karma vs. oak trees!

How do we distinguish "driven" from "facilitated" as an internal process?! I'm not sure how our still-limited human brains would suss out the difference. Along those lines, I could venture that the karmic trajectories of *our* individual lives—yours and mine—have driven us to this juncture where our respective daimons are facilitating whatever emerges as *Images of Soul: Reimagining Astrology.*

Here we are with all those letters we exchanged way back then, exploring what they might be trying to grow into between us now. I can't help noting that, in addition to the transits and progressions in our own charts, we're approaching the Saturn return of our initial correspondence—time to take what we've learned and integrate it, mature it. I can take what you just said in your email about Frederich and apply it to what we're doing here: "The archetype of Chronos /Saturn has cleared the way for the past (Saturn) to become an embodied, concrete, real, part of the present. I have a feeling there will be some kind of resolution…" Has psyche presented you with an image for that yet?

From: Judie
To: Hadley
Subject: Emergence

I've recently begun reading Sonu Shamdasani's dialogue with James Hillman in *Lament of the Dead*. I'm barely into it, and I've been impacted tremendously. I've been led back into my own personal ancestry in order to reflect upon so many things: personal, psychological and archetypal—all unexplained, and unaccounted for. Questions emerged. Are these themes reincarnational? Is this the reason for so many eccentric, unexplained personal and interpersonal behavioral and psychological patterns? The term "lament" in the title of the book seems so fitting. I've experienced a kind of haunting my entire life: of themes, people, whose very presence seemed to exist from the time I was barely four years old. I don't espouse reincarnation as such, but there is a reincarnating *feeling* about this. Almost as if the soul, possessing the same characteristics, passes from one person, one embodiment, to another.

From: Hadley
To: Judie
Subject: Emergence

I have an image of the daimon slipping into one skin suit after another!

Some months back I heard a radio interview with a rabbi. The subject was the afterlife, and he was asked if there was a Jewish principle of reincarnation. He said that was normally associated with the more mystical teachings of the Kabbalah. He talked about a nighttime prayer in which one is supposed to say: "I hereby forgive those who did this and this" because you're supposed to go to sleep forgiving people. Then he said there was a line in that prayer, which clearly has those mystical roots. It adds: "...and forgive those who have hurt me, whether in this incarnation or in a previous incarnation." Perhaps something in your ancestry knows about that even if you don't consciously espouse it?

From: Judie
To: Hadley
Subject: Emergence

Who knows? The topic of ancestors seems to be gaining current popularity in depth psychology circles. I believe Jung wrote extensively about it way back. There does seem to be something important to it, besides the obvious physiological links. I can't help thinking there are archetypal family patterns needing attention. I've seen these patterns exist in family members' horoscopes, person to person, family members to family members. What do these images of soul— often seen as haunting family themes—want from us? For me that question itself has become a kind of haunting . Of course these concerns are more than personal. More than just my little concern, my haunting. Could it be that the lament of our personal hauntings wants to be given as an offering to the soul of the world?

I had a short dream recently, in which I held onto four monarch butterflies all connected by a string. They ranged from large to small. I knew I must release these images of psyche/soul—i.e., butterflies—out into the world. I opened a window and let them fly free, thus releasing soul into the world. Since that dream, my normally introverted self has a much greater urge to participate in more extraverted activities of the outer world.

From: Hadley
To: Judie
Subject: Emergence

That's a gorgeous image! There's also a hint of the butterfly effect and String Theory in there, but that's an exploration for another time. As for the issue of hauntings and ancestors, there's that old saying in family systems work: "Emotional systems are not fooled by time, distance, or death." And you just beautifully addressed the enigma around reincarnation. Again, our human consciousness has to use the brain to steer us toward the mystery, so for those of us who use the lens of Evolutionary Astrology in our work, we can only conceptualize what that "looks" like in terms of how our current life is unfolding. I suspect there's a much more dimensional picture than that.

You're also speaking to one aspect of my master's thesis on "Astrology & Family Systems" as well as to what I saw in my work when I was back east. For all the challenges I encountered, I did get to do (with several co-therapists) group family therapy—sometimes with three generations in each of 6-8 families in the room at one time. I had stacks of charts to work with before the families arrived and found them, of course, invaluable. When we use a derivative chart method to see the psychic imprint on the individual from 2-3 generations back, "haunting" is a very apt concept—I wish I'd had it in my psyche at the time. I certainly saw it play out, though.

From: Judie
To: Hadley
Subject: Pondering

I've been meaning to sculpt those butterflies and hang them on the patio as wind chimes. The problem I have is if they stay connected and remain wind chimes, then they're not flying free. Perhaps they need to be made one at a time and then hung in varying heights close to one another. Ah, I think I've just figured it out. Keep the connection but not the tie or enmeshment so close that it inhibits freedom of individual movement. Perhaps this would be a good idea also within family systems! But then I digress.

So here we are, talking a lot here about astrology, but we're not just counseling astrologers. We're both licensed psychotherapists. How does that figure into what we're proposing as the next wave in both fields, into what we each see as hugely worthy of consideration by colleagues and clients in both fields? I'm asking a question out loud! I have thoughts, or maybe they're only assumptions and hopes.

It seems inevitable that the astrological/mythical language will be seen as more and more relevant with each passing year. Look at the quality of books on the subject and how current astrological thought and practice are becoming more and more mythological, psychological, transpersonal, and reincarnational with each year. The level of astrology has been raised in a contemporary sense way beyond anything I'd originally imagined when I'd first started writing my dissertation. And there's even more to come. This feels like more than just a temporary renaissance. There's also a linkage with what's become an increasingly higher caliber among those in the arts, quantum physics, practitioners of depth psychology, etc.

From: Hadley
To: Judie
Subject: Emergence

Yes! Long ago Richard [Idemon] urged me to hold on to what Stanford emeritus professor William Tiller had said: "Mathematics will continue to be the quantitative language of science, but astrology will become the qualitative language of the human condition." In those early days, even dear friends thought I'd gone 'round the bend, and my then-husband concurred. So, when *you* went back to school, I was at last not the only astrologer I knew who'd bet her future on the belief that astrology would someday be of tremendous importance to the field of psychology—that the two were a natural enhancement to one another!

Again though, through all the years, we've both known our first responsibility as therapists and as astrologers is to the client's particular issues and needs in the here and now. An accurate and insightful assessment of that amalgam comes from the years of experience in both fields. And I, for one, am so grateful to see more and more astrologers pulling away from the descriptive, reductionistic model that says, "You're such-and-such a sign and therefore...." Or "you have this-and-that configuration in your chart, so you'll always...." To me, this current evolution makes it increasingly possible to expand and explore the ways the two arts can work together.

Also, in my thirty-plus years as a licensed therapist, this past decade of work has revealed one increasingly consistent yearning: clients are on the search for meaning, for the understanding of personal challenges, patterns, and complexes on a more transrational level—that restoration of value to the soul that Hillman spoke about. Thus we have a challenge and a dilemma: lest there be an unproductive "flight into light," we know it's essential to do the intense earthly, psychological grunt work. Yet, as a colleague suggested years ago, if the therapist isn't watchful, the cultural pathologizing of that work (the list of DSM diagnoses seems endless) has as much chance of limiting the client's evolution as facilitating it. And, as astrologers, experience tells us there's the concomitant danger of truncating the client's internally-rooted, gradual, and congruent self-discovery when *too* much astrological insight is proffered. So, the Saturnian alembic is vital for alchemizing earthly progress and spiritual evolution.

From: Judie
To: Hadley
Subject: Emergence

Agreed! You know, although he's responsible for our meeting one another, I didn't know Richard at all well, but you reactivated his great spirit for me just now. As one of our astrological ancestors I take great pride in standing upon his shoulders, and I know how important he was as a mentor to you.

And I've been thinking about how we might differentiate between our two methods. Could we say that, in my case, I see the horoscope as being the container of mythic images that lead the way and describe the journey of a soul from acorn to oak (in Hillman's terms)? As I reflect upon it, I'm not at all sure we're that different. Both ways of working seem to interpenetrate and offer to the other something of value. In your case, is it that the evolutionary astrologer's theory and practice are seen as an exploration of the challenges and lessons in each lifetime vs. the challenges and lessons in a horoscope that can be seen as asking for completion in an evolutionary sense, lifetime to lifetime?

From: Hadley
To: Judie
Subject: Perspective[s]

I just don't see any "vs." in there. As you described in your table of astrological perspectives there are parallels between all the approaches. And astrology is such an elegant overarching system—it can hold in its embrace the entirety of everything you just articulated. To call on an image or two here: we're all playing notes in a vast cosmic symphony; or we'll all dots in a cosmic pointillist painting. Or, in the words of Ram Dass: "We're all just walking each other home."

From: Judie
To: Hadley
Subject: Perspective[s]

Ah Ram Dass! How I love him. If you haven't see his film "Fierce Grace," I highly recommend it as one of the requirements for anyone doing any counseling with another human being. The last part where he works with a young woman is not to be missed. It should be a requirement in order to get the state MFT license.

Getting back to my table of astro-psychological perspectives. Yes! I used that table to show that horoscopes are interpreted, and their purpose lived, from lower to higher levels of sophistication. The various perspectives can all be seen as blueprints of potential, each with lesser-to-greater degrees of sophistication. There's an interpenetration of some kind going on all the time between all the astro-psychological perspectives. I know it can be confusing, but ultimately the move is toward the ideal, toward imagination. I suspect the ultimate expression would be some kind of amalgamation of all of the perspectives.

For now, though, who could've imagined Hillman would have such a commercial success with the material in *The Soul's*

Code? Back in the day, I didn't have even a hint that what I'd entitled The Imaginal Perspective would become so damned meaningful and still be so alive for me today. And when I say alive, I mean personally, clinically *alive!* Only now I'm even more attracted. More hooked. I'm more immersed in the whole metaphor of a daimon, an acorn, in charge of a full-on destiny. Both of us see that destiny etched onto the chart wheel—where the archetypal complexes are configured geometrically and compose the face of a horoscope. They translate into images, into mythic patterns of story telling, and the progressed movement forward or backward in time unfolds in the ultimate living out of these various inner and outer dramas of our life stories, otherwise known as the images of soul.

From: Hadley
To: Judie
Subject: Perspective[s]

Actually, I was so moved by "Fierce Grace" that I bought the video, and I agree with you on all counts!

Not to make too fine a point: I also see the full-on destiny, those mythic patterns, laid out in that chart as part of an ongoing evolutionary pattern.

From: Judie
To: Hadley
Subject: One more question

Oh, of course these patterns also compose an ongoing evolutionary system. Perhaps myth is the language through which our evolutionary patterns speak and our life stories are told, lifetime to lifetime. Maybe one more question as we wind down. What do you think: does the daimon design the horoscope? (Couldn't resist that one!)

From: Hadley
To: Judie
Subject: One more question

Let's imagine that's so! Jean Houston refers to it as rediscovering "our Essence" and that rediscovery leads to "our greatness," which is the daimon's intent and the idea behind Jung's individuation.

From: Judie
To: Hadley
Subject: One more question

Interesting that you refer to her. I just put down a book on quantum physics; she has a chapter in it that describes the exact same thing. I, too, drew an instant parallel between Houston's ideas and *The Soul's Code*. As astrologers we both want our clients to get closer to their essence(s) and as psychotherapists we want the same for our patients—i.e., to get closer to what, in Maslow's language, is their actualized self. Among the many wonderful things about astrology is that, when you bring to bear all possibilities within an astrological session, you can help guide clients via the astrological map to those aspects of the self and the personal world that most enhance and illuminate their very particular journey.

From: Hadley
To: Judie
Subject: One more question

That calls to mind Hillman's "Anima Mundi" essay, in which he writes: "If we could reoriginate psychology ... a way might open again toward a meta-psychology that is a cosmology, a poetic vision of the cosmos which fulfills the soul's need for placing itself in the vast scheme of things."[13] To me, his life seemed devoted to reminding those in our field of the enormous value of the psyche-logical! Might I imagine, my friend, that you concur?!

From: Judie
To: Hadley
Subject: Okay, more than one more question

I concur with great delight! And that delight that takes me right back to the role of the evolutionary astrologer. Is there an equivalent to the soul's code, to the daimon's work, in your astrological process with clients?

---

[13] Hillman, James, *The Thought of the Heart & the Soul of the World,* Spring Publications, Woodstock, CT, 1997, pp. 109-110

From: Hadley
To: Judie
Subject: Okay, more than one more question

We could call it Imaginal Evolutionary Astrobiology! The chart is the third dimensional diagram of the daimon's work—its genome—in this lifetime. I can't see it any other way.

To use an extremely reductionistic example, if the daimon comes in with the "mission" to learn how to dance, that's the issue regardless of whether it's a tango, waltz, ballet, hip-hop, flamenco, belly, etc. All of these conjure very different images, yet the core issue is the "learn to dance" acorn. Or if someone had a karmic task that involved learning how to use language, s/he could conceivably do that by becoming a writer, public speaker, translator, sign language interpreter; by giving voice to anyone who has none; by overcoming a personal speaking disability, etc. Evolutionary Astrology looks at the daimon's mission and seeks to elucidate what from the karmic past might get in the way of fulfilling it as well as what might be used to facilitate its fullest possible realization.

As I've said previously, it seems to me that images come to *you* directly from the imaginal realm in a rather reliable way; but my particular psyche doesn't operate quite like that. Some time back I mentioned integrating Lauren Schneider's Tarotpy system into my sessions. I love her method of using many different tarot and other card decks with an enormous interpretive range and variety of archetypal images on them to help someone see the chart in visual terms. And not only to explore the chart, but also to address an issue that may arise in a therapy session and could benefit from the transrational perspective the images catalyze. When we separate ourselves from the traditional meanings of the cards and focus solely on the images, it's fascinating to experience how they give us the story, the synchronicity—highlight the patterns that are showing up in the client's life right now. It's brought a new kind of dimensionality to my work, and I'm loving it. There are hundreds of decks available these days, and in Lauren's system the particular set or style of images to which one is drawn will somehow resonate with the deep wisdom and truth operating at a particular time in the client's unconscious.

No fortune telling here—I wouldn't even know how—but it's quite something to *see* how the archetypes are patterned and interacting with one another, and then have the client sit with them and describe to me what s/he is seeing in that mirror to the soul. What *I* see might be entirely different. As you've often noted, all images of soul have a life of their own, so regardless of what we think is the "source," when one (or several) enters any kind of session we're doing, there will be an effect of some kind, somewhere, somehow. It's not our business to know the earthly details of that effect, but there will be one. Surely, as much as anything, we both use images and stories to make it possible to sneak past egoic defense structures. So in a certain way, our astropsychological work helps reset the ego.

And for all of our contemplations and ruminations here, I'm forever mindful of Jung's oft-quoted admonition which I discovered in my first year of grad school: "Learn your theories as well as you can, but put them aside when you touch the miracle of the living soul. Not theories, but your creative individuality alone must decide."

From: Judie
To: Hadley
Subject: Endings

Quite fitting to end with the wisdom of that particular ancestor.

PART 5

So How Does It All Work?

The Meeting of Imaginal and Evolutionary Perspectives

It's better to fail therapeutically than to fail humanly.

-- Robert Stein[14] in conversation with Judie

We've selected this particular case study because, in real life and in full human detail, cases sometimes don't wrap up as tidily as astrologers and clinicians might wish. The acorn sprouts, the daimon reaches out, but the ego restricts the amount of sun and rain available. Nonetheless, the choice is always there as Rilke notes in his poem "Archaic Torso of Apollo." The concluding words—"for here there is no place/that does not see you. You must change your life"—are the perfect example of a daimon's moment. Rilke has engaged the power of what's in front of him and tries to name it, but he's aware of the limitation of words and realizes he must choose to make a leap on another level. We believe that the

---

[14] Stein, Robert, M.D., Jungian analyst, author of *Incest and Human Love*

joining of the imaginal and evolutionary perspectives can be an invaluable part of making that leap possible. The operative word is "choice."

Mark and the Mystery Woman: A Case Study

Judie: Mark had been my psychotherapy patient on and off for two years. He's a writer in his early 60s and prone to many of the things working writers in Hollywood suffer amidst the ups and downs of their profession. He's a lovely, charming man at his core and the divorced father of two children in their 20s.

His thrust in life focuses in two directions: his work and his painfully ambivalent, red-hot obsession with visions of a captivating creature whom he'd actually met only once several years ago when she sat next to him on a transatlantic flight. They'd had, by his report, a profound conversation that ended after many hours only because the plane landed. He tried to contact her soon after that, but the information she'd given him turned out to be incorrect; the people who answered the phone had never heard of her. His recurring memory of her in a long black dress and cape haunted him relentlessly. She had exited the plane and his life in a single instant, but this costume remained an imprinted part of Mark's imaginal fantasies.

He has very pleasant exchanges with women, dates here and there, but no woman has ever lived up to his fantasies about what life could be like with this mystery woman. This wouldn't be unusual with Neptune in Libra in the

7th house—the idealized "other"—but much in his chart also inclines him to encounter women in a non-attached way. Other than a brief marriage and the children he loves, there seemed to be some nagging concern that's kept him from emotionally consummating any relationship. His Moon-Mercury conjunction in Capricorn in the 10th house opposite Uranus in Cancer in the 4th speaks to this specifically and to the relationships in his life coming and going in general. He also comes and goes in therapy and can't seem to settle. I began to think that, because he could at least have *her*, he didn't want to "share" her despite the frustration. With all the Piscean and Sagittarian energy in the chart, there was also something deeply spiritual in him, but nothing I knew of in his life suggested he was living that in any obvious way. His writing earned him a good living, but he never spoke of it in terms of inspiration.

After carefully ascertaining the absence of psychopathology, and other than suspecting a touch of Asperger's, in the first year, I explored with him all the usual methods of engaging this elusive creature—i.e., taking of personal history, dream work, written/verbal imaginal dialogues, story telling, etc. As in most therapeutic interactions, there was progress in fits and starts. Degrees of opening, backtracking, opening again. He would come to the brink of awareness, like Rilke, but jump back from the daimon's "You must change your life" gaze. He seemed stuck in something. It resembled what's called a "redintegration loop" wherein the intense memory would move in on him like a dream, he could let it go for a time, then something would inevitably trigger its return.

What astropsychological sense are we to make of the archetypal complex in Mark's chart? The configuration of Venus in Sagittarius in the 9th house sets the stage for his relationship with this figure (intriguing foreign female residing somewhere abroad, met on an airplane). Then we see the ruler Jupiter in Pisces in the 12th house of archetypes of the collective unconscious; Jupiter has domain rulership not only over his Venus but also over his Sagittarian Sun and Chiron in the 9th.

Clearly this configuration has inclined him to long for, chase, mourn, and be overwhelmed by a spiritualized, wounding, feminine archetype. Does this burst of fiery Sagittarian energy in the 9th want to be lived out more as an archetype and journey of the imagination than as a life with a real woman? And what of the image of the maternal feminine, Mark's Capricorn Moon in the 10th house? So far he seems to have embraced the benefits and successes of his lucrative career rather than opening himself to a full-on loving relationship with a woman in real life. When his mystery woman exited the plane all those years ago, she carried something of Mark with her. Is the story to end there?

Feeling the need for the infusion of another clinical perspective after a particularly frustrating session for both Mark and myself, I took a risk and explained to him how Hadley works. I suggested we consult with her to see if something of clinical value might be uncovered through an evolutionary astropsychological perspective. Somewhat to my surprise, he agreed to this, signed an information release form, even seemed slightly excited and encouraged for a few moments. Then came his hand-on-the-door declaration that he really was terribly busy right now and would accept Hadley's input in writing, but not in an in-person meeting.

His rigid declaration sent my antenna way up. Given the dynamics in his horoscope I now suspected he was in the life-long grip of the kind of archetypal complex Richard Tarnas refers to as functioning like "an enclosing wall, an impermeable boundary and barrier that effectively creates a limit to our universe of possibilities."[15] I also wondered when and if "a critical awareness of that particular boundary [along with] an act of the imagination to transcend it,"[16] could be accessed so that the "horizon of [Mark's] universe,"[17] could in fact be opened. Critical questions had to be readdressed within myself. Was Mark's life meant to be opened? Was this *my* agenda for Mark? As a health care provider and soul-caretaker it's difficult not to humanly have this expectation, and yet I had to look deeply into those places where his and my psychological concerns may have crossed and interpenetrated.

Given my take on this recalcitrant archetypal complex, could an astrological past life picture provide any further illumination about this current intriguing, dark, female presence in Mark's inner life? Since his outer life encounter with the actual woman was so brief, surely his obsession was more about his daimon than about her. I couldn't help

---

[15] Tarnas, Richard. *Cosmos and Psyche: Intimations of a New World View*, Viking-Penguin Group, 2006, p. 292
[16] Tarnas, Ibid.,
[17] Tarnas, Ibid.,

wondering if this was yet another long, frustrating turn in the road orchestrated for some mysterious reason by his daimon. What was this avoidance—which was then immediately literalized by his having to be on location for the next six months? Was it time for me to take a look at my own process and countertransference position around this issue and examine my own personal resonances in this area?

Nevertheless, I was encouraged by the openness he could muster for what, to him, seemed like an avant garde idea, so I called Hadley and asked for a consultation. I felt that, at the very least, Mark deserved and very much needed whatever illumination my colleague might be able to provide, one that I hoped I could eventually pass along to him.

~ ~ ~ ~ ~ ~ ~ ~ ~ ~ ~ ~ ~

Hadley offered Judie the following impressions with the reminder that this interpretive overview wasn't necessarily a true story, but that on a soul level, it would be an accurate one for this chart:

Hadley: Using some basic components of the evolutionary approach to this chart gives me the outline of a story that would involve Mark being a priest in the karmic past—a kind of Abelard figure. It's likely he'd always believed he had a powerful calling to the religious life; and from the beginning he'd insisted quite firmly on a nearly inhuman standard of adherence to religious ideals at the expense of the natural connections of ordinary human life.

So let us imagine that, as a result, he gained status and reached an elevated position in the parish and religious community in which he functioned. Possibly an arrogance with regard to his own "achievements" developed over time as the powers-that-be began to know who he was, and he garnered admiration from the people to whom he ministered. We might even muse that, regardless of when he lived historically (I envision something around the 17th century), he might've viewed the precepts of the Inquisition as an efficient way for the Church to maintain good discipline! I'm referring so far (basically) to his Saturn in Libra in the out-of-sign conjunction with the south node in Virgo in the 7th house and Saturn's ruler Venus in Sagittarius conjunct the Sun in the 9th house and squaring the nodal structure across the horizon. (Notice that the Moon, Mercury, Mars, and Uranus all *ultimately* disposit to that Saturn in Libra which rules the Moon, Mars, and Mercury all at the top of the chart.) I think the memory of this religious calling—and what we might now call its consequences—is deep in his psyche even now.

Perhaps he was able to maintain his secure position for quite some time—until, my imagining self suggests, the local order of nuns bring into their community a new sister who'd temporarily been assigned to help them work with the children in the parish school which Mark oversees. The dispositing triad of Venus in Sagittarius, Neptune in Libra, and Jupiter in Pisces not only points to aspects of his complex in this lifetime, but can also let us surmise that this nun's entire demeanor was graceful, otherworldly. We could see her moving about with focused ease doing her work and exuding a joyful commitment to her calling. Surely, her black habit covered every part of her body; but her white wimple could have highlighted an exotic, unforgettable face.

Maybe he was quickly overwhelmed with romantic ideations and erotic feelings utterly foreign to him, feelings that soon abducted him into an enormous internal struggle. Anything other than the professional contact between these two people would've been forbidden on every conceivable level, and it's likely she was devoutly firm—though gracious—in evading his attempts to develop their relationship in any way.

When she was sent away to another convent (I don't have a sense of the timeline here, but the 9th house Venus and Chiron in Sagittarius in wide square to Saturn is one aspect of suggesting this loss), he no doubt felt bereft and wounded. What he loved wounded him. Could we imagine that he never recovered from the loss, that he may have become ill and/or felt embittered regarding what he came to see as the Church's power to afflict his human heart? (I'm looking here at the Venus-Chiron-Sun conjunction in Sagittarius square the nodal structure and south node ruler Mercury conjunct the Moon in Capricorn opposite the 12th house ruler Uranus in Cancer in the 4th).

I can't know if that long-lost nun was indeed reincarnated as the woman he saw on the plane all those years ago, but I suspect her black gown and cape and her exotic appearance awakened that unresolved archetypal experience in his psyche. Of course she's still unattainable, but what if she's haunting him now to awaken him and serve as muse in some way?

He may not be ill or overtly bitter in this lifetime, but, dear friend, your description of his (not) romantic life suggests he's still got work to do in the "human" realm. Certainly that could mean making an actual adult relationship work—including his relationship with you! But it could also mean that this time around he needs to experience *himself* as "beautiful," and be known for the work inspired by his deep inner muse, known for possessing his own creativity and elegance.

I wonder what kinds of opportunities he has to do any of this in "the business"? It seems like his current life keeps him emotionally safe in ways not far afield of what the Church provided in a less benign way in the karmic past. I hope he returns to work with you. The years are ticking away, but if what I've said here has any meaning for him, there's still time to do some rewrites on his own story. He might do well to explore the conscious development of a truly meaningful spiritual life, too. As Caroline Casey noted years ago, "The health of the visible depends upon the health of the invisible force field that surrounds it."[18]

Also, prior to his own internal revisioning, he may first need to speak of and accept his worst, chronic fear that in fact he may never again in this lifetime experience the kind of attraction that seized him in flight(!). If Mark *could* make this kind of emotional descent it might catalyze and mirror an inner psychological state in which he could recommit to his

---

[18] Casey, Caroline W. *Making the Gods Work for You: The Astrological Language of the Psyche,* Harmony Books, New York, 1998, p.61

work with you in what, for him, would truly be the rich alchemical dung.

~ ~ ~ ~ ~ ~ ~ ~ ~ ~ ~ ~ ~

Possible Outcome: Factoring in the evolutionary story, what might additional psychotherapy offer by way of exploring Mark's recalcitrant archetypal complex of Sun, Venus, Jupiter, etc.? The ideal would be to bring into the room all latent possibilities that could provide him with a deeper understanding of his love for *his* mystery woman, all the while bearing in mind the mysterious, unknown trajectory coveted by, and held in the capable hands of, his daimon who may, in fact, have its own agenda!

In Conclusion

He who is born in imagination discovers the latent forces of Nature.... Besides the stars that are established, there is yet another—Imagination— that begets a new star and a new heaven.

-- Paracelsus

Evolution is inherent in the image of the acorn. Its internal timepiece moves it along a trajectory toward "oakness." Depending on all sorts of ecological determinants, it will transform into some version of an oak tree, whether minor or magnificent—the symbolic equivalent of some baser metal or of alchemical gold.

Similarly, by reimagining astrology, by more closely connecting to the myriad components of our horoscopic patterning via our own images of soul, we have seen how our daimon's unique trajectory inclines us toward fulfilling our evolutionary purpose. The *amalgam of birth chart, images of soul, daimon's trajectory, and circuitous evolutionary path* brings us closer and closer to the source of our own alchemical gold.

We continue to notice the impact that reimagining astrology has had in our own lives and in the lives of clients and patients. There is little doubt in our minds, hearts, and souls that when the astrological experience is reimagined, it deepens the experience of astrological counseling for both client and practitioner. We hope that by our bringing back to life and elaborating upon some of these quietly slumbering ideas, they—and you, our readers—might find new purpose within the current astropsychological time-space continuum.

When myth and images are used to explore, amplify, and unearth the astrological patterns inherent within a horoscope, that horoscope becomes a container of unimaginable depth. Within that container, what Hillman describes in *The Soul's Code* as the soul's fate, its particular path, may be held, perceived, explored, and achieved *in depth*. This, in turn, makes it possible to raise the level of astrological understanding, as hinted at by Tarnas, either during the course of this lifetime, or, if viewed from the position of Evolutionary Astrology, over the course of many.

We believe that the material and ideas presented in this book can offer, at the very least, small insights into the ways that the level of astrological psychology has indeed been—and will continue to be—"raised."

We are eternally grateful to Richard Tarnas for *that* thought of his heart.

PART 6

Comparative Astropsychological Perspectives

Note to the reader: Many years have passed since Judie conceptualized and integrated these comparative tables of astropsychological perspectives as part of her doctoral dissertation. As we neared the completion of our book, she felt this one area remained incomplete. She saw a need to underline in greater depth the potential value, to both client and astroconsultant within an astrological session (and time and money permitting), of actually applying one or more of the astropsychological perspectives described in the tables on the following pages. Think of it as similar to the process of making a painting, writing a poem, or crafting a sculpture— i.e., a client comes for a chart analysis, and more than what was expected emerges. Judie saw it as the weaving of additional dimensions and perspectives, strand by strand as a way of augmenting the client's past, present, and/or future life experience and perspective. So she set about imagining what these extended sessions might look like.

For example, in one part of a session the chart analysis might require a more concrete interpretation, dialogue, and feedback. In this case a sound, grounded use of astrological theory and practice would come into play. The astrological consultant would draw from a solid elementary background as s/he applied a well-schooled foundation in the basics during the session. It would be akin to the best, earthiest, tastiest version of Mom's astrological apple pie made by astrologers such as Robert Hand, Lee Lehman, or Robert Zoller.

Or, in another astrological session, the transits might indicate that the client is moving into an enhanced, meditative, transpersonal phase of life. The astrological consultant might add another layer and incorporate into the session the discussion of meditation or other spiritual practices or suggest these be factored into the client's life. Astrologer and client might sit and meditate together or listen to a recording that facilitates mindfulness. The astroconsultant could recommend reading material relevant to this current phase in the client's life. As indicators that it is indeed time to integrate this approach, the transits would lead the way and provide more specific assistance.

Or the client and astroconsultant might together explore the client's evolutionary trajectory by drawing focus to the transpersonal planets and the nodal axis and mutually exploring how the karmic past could be impacting or contributing to the client's present life direction and purpose. Recommending works by Dane Rudhyar, Stephen Forrest, or Jeffrey Wolf Green would be appropriate in this case.

Or the client might bring a dream—or a description of a dream might emerge—during a session. The astropsychological consultant who is conversant with mythological story and the concepts contained in Jung's psychology could encourage discussion of Jungian dream interpretation or of the ways the astrological elements and qualities relate to Jung's typology. The incorporation of these aspects of Jungian thought would deepen the experience for both. When activated by transit or progression, major natal planetary configurations (or archetypal complexes) that are asking for exploration could also be examined by adding a bit of the Jungian perspective. The recommendation of readings by C.G. Jung, Laurence Hillman, Liz Greene, or Richard Tarnas could further illuminate the Jungian astropsychological perspective.

And finally, through the use of images and the process of imaginal dialogue in a session, the astropsychological consultant and client might paint a series of word pictures not chosen in advance by either. With the astroconsultant acting as a guide in a trusting process of exploring the images, they would together explore and illuminate archetypal planetary complexes and life concerns. The surprises that emerge without a specific agenda might lead both client and astroconsultant back through the past, deeper into the present, and/or toward a more realized, consciously lived future. The work of Richard Tarnas, Brad Kochunas, James Hillman and Thomas Moore would merit recommendation here.

Obviously, the application of all of these perspectives at once would be overwhelming, and any one of them may not be necessary or may not work for a particular client—and above all, the astroconsultant is there to serve the needs of the client. However, for some, when drawing from the essence of one or two perspectives, the use of small parts of each can enrich and deepen a consultation far beyond what either the client or the astropsychological consultant could've imagined. *Clearly, this would not be considered or defined as psychotherapy unless engaged in at the direction of a licensed professional.*

Drawing from one or more perspectives would be much like crafting an astropsychological collage. The astrological consultant would offer a stream of meaning, impressions regarding the depth of dreams, articulations of the richness of mythic story, and/or perhaps the exploration of how certain aspects of one's existence in prior lifetimes are woven together here and now within the realities of this contemporary, everyday world. Once understood, these various perspectives provide a context for what came before and how, as in Hadley's work, we might use experiences of the karmic past to more deeply understand and enrich our relationships and perspective in this lifetime.

The presentation of possibilities for deepening the experience of the astropsychological counseling process found within these multiple perspectives is meant to guide our readers toward a deeper understanding of the lessons, gifts, and failings inherent in their *past* while seeking to enrich the myriad dimensions of their *future.*

We offer this table of comparative astropsychological perspectives, in which each perspective is divided into theory and process, in order to help illuminate the experience of those who wish to encounter on a deeper level what we believe to be the magical meeting place of spirit, image, and soul that is carefully cloistered in that circle of eternal mystery, the astrological horoscope. With its inner time-keeper and the pulse of our daimon's instructions, it is where *we've* placed our psychological faith; and, given patience and time, we believe it can lead each of us to our calling in this lifetime.

TRADITIONAL PERSPECTIVE: Theory

First Principle: To forecast

Orientation: Event-focused

Style of Interaction: To see and to believe

Astrology as: A cosmic science and statement of universal order, a tool to measure and assess character and personality qualities, a view of microcosmic and macrocosmic correspondences

Birth Horoscope as: A causal plan of predetermined human destiny and/or reincarnational pattern

In this perspective, the astrologer is the ultimate authority with all the answers. The client seeks his/her approval and direction for important decisions. The astrologer acts like a parent figure sought out for definitive guidance as to life direction, particularly regarding the timing of past, present, and future events.

TRADITIONAL PERSPECTIVE: Process

Language as:	Reductive cause and effect statements, deterministic dictums, fortune telling, magic
Words as:	Oracles
Mode of Participation:	Linear, archetypal roles: parent-child, seer-believer
Outcome:	Satisfy personal curiosity, attempt to predict and control past, present and future (reincarnational) lifetimes, reinforce (outer) social and gender roles, escape personal responsibility, forecast and time life events
Astrological Theorists:	Bailey, Baker, Hickey, Hone, Jacobson, Leo, Moore and Douglas, Pagan, Sakoian and Acker

This event-perspective parallels a Freudian transference/countertransference experience in psychotherapy. Just as the patient might turn to a Freudian analyst as all-knowing, parentified figure, so might the astrological client see the astrological consultant as someone who has all the answers. The horoscope and ephemeris become the ultimate authorities from which to gain permission—or not—related to timing and when to take action. The relationship is a dependent one; the astrologer and the horoscope are the ultimate source of answers.

HUMANISTIC PERSPECTIVE: Theory

First Principle:	To realize
Orientation:	Person-focused
Style of Interaction:	To inspire and to awaken
Astrology as:	A tool or vehicle for the actualization of human potential, a marriage of astrological structure and psychological content
Birth Horoscope as:	A blueprint of cyclically unfolding human potential, an inherently whole seed pattern

As astrology became more humanistic, so did the way in which astrological client and humanistic astrologer engaged one another. While not completely without prediction, the astrologer was more interested in helping the clients find and engage their human potential. Life events and experiences were likened to the unfolding patterns of a seed out of which the individual would grow, out of which human potential could flourish. This was not unlike a guiding daimon or image of soul. The astrologer's analysis of the birth horoscope might focus upon transits and progressions as parts of cycles highlighting those times when self-actualization was likely to be most possible.

HUMANISTIC PERSPECTIVE: Process

Language as:	Personal, psychological and human encouragement, direction, "coaching" and inspiration, provider of content about what experiences are necessary to actualize birth potential
Words as:	Catalysts and transformers
Mode of Participation:	Cyclic, holistic, heroic, athletic and transcendent, archetypal role: coach-athlete
Outcome:	Broaden and enlarge psychological consciousness, "growth," problem solving, assume personal responsibility, personal and social transformation, clinical implications for humanistic and transpersonal psychology, spiritual enlightenment
Astrological Theorists:	Arroyo, Dobyns, Hand, Huber, Jones, Lundsted, Mayo, Meyer, Oken, Idemon, Forrest, Rudhyar, Tyl
Psychological Theorists:	Maslow, Rogers, Psychology's third force

In the humanistic encounter, the sky's the limit. Interaction between astrologer and client is with heads turned upward. The astrologer aims for the heights in order to help clients be the best and most they can be. Client and astrologer are on a quest for spirit. "Actualize, actualize, actualize" is their mantra. There is opening and possibility. The client finally has something to say about the process. "Growth" is the goal in all areas, humanly and spiritually.

JUNGIAN PERSPECTIVE: Theory

First Principle: To analyze

Orientation: Meaning-focused

Style of Interaction: To guide and to journey

Astrology as: A language having symbolic, conceptual and typological correlation to the psychology of C. G. Jung, an astro-psychological pathway of the individuation process

Birth Horoscope as: A map of the psychological heaven within and symbol of the Self archetype

Things begin to quiet down—and deepen and darken—in this perspective. Language is tenanted by the gods—mostly Greek, but often from other countries, such as India, Ireland, etc. The planets suddenly afford the opportunity to be viewed in the context of their Greek origins. One's Venus square Saturn is richer when seen as an archetypal complex, and then the mythic story behind this square is re-visited. Here the astrologer, who is often a psychotherapist or analyst, is apt to be seen in the role of psychological guide.

JUNGIAN PERSPECTIVE: Process

Language as:	Education, understanding, interpretive analogies between astrology, mythology, and Jungian psychology
Words as:	Symbols and concepts
Mode of Participation:	Bi-modal: light, detached, rational and/or dark, intense, chaotic Archetypal roles: guide-traveler, teacher-student
Outcome:	Perceive the relationship between an outer event and an inner psychological image, serve consciousness as unconscious contents become conscious, serve "Self," transformation of symbols, clinical implications for depth psychology and astrology
Astrological Theorists:	Greene, Hamaker-Zondag, Howell, Sasportas, Guttman, L. Hillman, G. Perry, D. George, G. Bogart
Psychological Theorists:	Jung

The analysis of dreams plays a part in the interplay of astrologer and client. The horoscope is seen and discussed symbolically and mythically. Astrological symbols come to life via dreams and life events. Meaning is found when astrological transits are seen to unlock, reveal, and illuminate the archetypal complexes that comprise the psychological dynamics of the natal astrological aspects.

IMAGINAL PERSPECTIVE: Theory

First Principle: To imagine

Orientation: Image-focused

Style of Interaction: To explore and to discover

Astrology as: A system of images, an art ritual, locus of the soul's woundedness, the experience and expression of multiple forms of consciousness

Birth Horoscope as: An archetypal model of life or soul, an artist's palette, container of individual genius, a source of images and a round of planetary deities

On our exploration here, the only map we have is the horoscope. Shouldn't that be enough? Despite the *apparent* structure of the horoscope, with its dynamics, its aspects, planets, signs, etc., we are called upon to seek more, to be open to more. Our faith is to be placed in the images that originate and arise from the horoscope and from the dialogue between astro-consultant and client during the session.

IMAGINAL PERSPECTIVE: Process

Language as:
Word paintings, an experiential and mutual process of imaginal dialogues, myth-making, story-telling

Words as:
Angels (message bearers), echoes, metaphor, image-carriers, containers of psyche, conveyors of soul

Mode of Participation:
Omni-directional, circular, archetypal roles: multiple

Outcome:
Art as a model for astropsychology, the entrance of a depth psychological and mutually experiential perspective within astropsychology, a polytheistic experience of the psyche/horoscope, transformation of images, clinical implications for depth psychology

Astrological Theorists:
Ficino, Poncé, Moore, Kochunas, Tarnas, Le Griece

Psychological Theorists:
Avens, Berry, Boer, Casey, Hillman, Watkins, Corbin

With our imaginations engaged, we are led to greater depths and possibly greater heights. We trust our acorn, its inner mechanism, and our daimon to guide us. Have we lived before? Maybe. We listen for soul's echo—and then talk back! We search for and find what we need when we write, paint, see, hear, experience, and know. We've only to place our faith in the images, and we can predict, plan, soar, analyze, or even revisit another lifetime. We journey in search of soul, vis-à-vis our horoscope, other images, and other imaginal places where we find all the gods present and accounted for.

Our Images Of Soul

Work of the eyes is done, now go and do heart-work on all the images imprisoned within you...

  -- Rilke, "Turning Point" trans. by Stephen Mitchell

One of the ways we serve the imagination is to become more interested in what we feel is part of our own acorn—and then to allow ourselves to be pulled toward that. Finding ways of interfacing with psyche, of expressing devotion to psyche and the imagination, needs no reason beyond the experience itself. It's a very healing thing to do.

In the elegant Publisher's Preface to *Healing Fiction* by James Hillman, George Quasha says:

> *As psychology grows scientistic, art becomes its unconscious .... In* psychology *psyche comes before logos, before the word and the telling, and this linguistic datum is suggestive in both the temporal sense of "being previous"—awaiting manifestation in what we can say—and in the spatial sense of "being in front"—getting into the foreground where service to the sayable is possible. What remains unsaid in us is forever angling to come into view; it seeks its art. Psyche and logos, soul and speech, psychology and poetics—Hillman*

wants us, the therapists and the poets (who once upon a time shared a single body), to see them as they are, inseparable, reflexive, and interdependent, and so to end one more hidden dualism that divides us from ourselves, our healing arts, and our sources.[19]

That's why we sculpt and write.

Brief examples of our creative work can be seen on the following pages.

---

[19] Hillman, *Healing Fiction*, op. cit. p. xi and xii

Judith's Sculptures

The Making of An "Offering"

In the world of poetry, if the title of a poem appears in the body of a poem, then that poem is often defined as an *ekphrasis*.

I'd been unaware of the term ekphrasis, until one day while sculpting. I'd taken a break, and while surfing the net, I stumbled upon ARAS's poetry portal where I gained further clarification about the term's poetic existence and definition. It was a lucky accident indeed. After realizing I'd unintentionally created an ekphrasis, I took the courageous step of submitting the poem to ARAS; it was accepted, and published online!

I'd not intended to write a poem, and certainly not one having such a complex definition. Yet when Psyche spoke, moving me to write intuitively as I sculpted, I listened. And soon, out of this mystery was born "Offering," a twenty-two inch soul figure having a curious resemblance to the way in which I've often imagined and seen my daimon.

Working on this figure has been rather like the circular process of Jung's psychological alchemy. One substance or state of soul morphed artistically into one form and then another until, finally, Psyche's angelic gift as *Offering* emerged out of Poseidon/Neptune's unconscious, sea-foamed swirl.

Judith Harte
2 February 2014

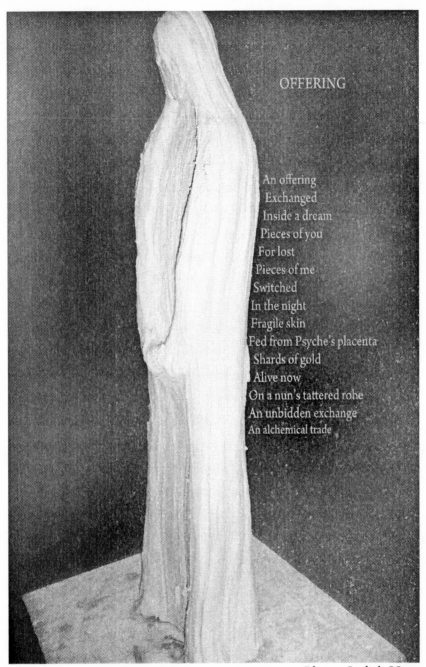

OFFERING

An offering
Exchanged
Inside a dream
Pieces of you
For lost
Pieces of me
Switched
In the night
Fragile skin
Fed from Psyche's placenta
Shards of gold
Alive now
On a nun's tattered robe
An unbidden exchange
An alchemical trade

Photo: Judith Harte

Hadley's Poetry

When a society becomes corrupt, what first grows gangrenous is language. Social criticism, therefore, begins with grammar and the reestablishment of meanings.... I believe the writer's attitude to language should be that of a lover....

— Octavio Paz, *The Labyrinth of Solitude*

Language was my first lover. That, perhaps, is the Irish in me.

Long before I could read, I'd steal into my parents' library when no one was watching and balance myself determinedly on my father's cushioned footstool. I would slide one book after another from its place, open it, and slowly rub my hand over the eggshell-colored pages, attempting to make sense of those small black symbols, trying to draw those words up through my skin and into my soul. I felt something—a life force—coming from them, and I desired them, wanted to know what they meant, wanted them *in* me. The images I needed came into me from the print on the page, like a spirit rising up to meet my own.

When I was five years old, my parents decided I should skip kindergarten in favor of first grade; they calmed my fears with a shameless bribe: first grade was where I would finally learn to read and write, and that meant I could find out what was in all those books in our house.

I started writing in earnest in high school, turned out essays and long letters over the years, then had several newspaper columns in the 1990s. I began writing poetry when I returned from my first and only visit to the land of my ancestors (in this incarnation). It was in Killarney in 1994 that I first heard David Whyte and the late John O'Donohue make prose so utterly poetic and poetry so utterly magical. Their words plus a personal encounter with another poetic Irishman re/minded me of a heritage from which I'd too long felt estranged.

Since we're well into this new millennium amidst a rapidly morphing techno-info-communication revolution, being "conscious" means—perhaps more than ever—making a commitment to the loving use of words, holding a reverence for their power in our hearts, being as aware as possible of how we use them in our exchanges with one another. Michael Meade put it very well: "The words from my mouth are beating on the drum of your ear, so don't think this is casual."

Hadley Fitzgerald
15 February 2014

When Dreams Were Chanted
by Hadley Fitzgerald

When dreams were chanted
magic worshipped
the goddess
light whispered
through mountains
and easy purple beauty
loved traveling
into the night

Now we lie frantic
so little music
hiding in dream water
storms sit
under the moon
asking
for her prayers
and gardens long
for our breath

Dancing with the Darkness
by Hadley Fitzgerald

You see the soul evolves
while we are busy making
other plans
Soul has no interest in what we want
or think we need
these times
they are a changin'
us
this time
and all our demons will drag
all our angels
to the center of The Room
to dance one last dance
All our selves are called
to put their arms around the partners
they have not wished to know
subject and object of God's loving quest
for Itself
to add our light to the sum of Light
and our love to the sum of Love

In this dance
we are allowed
one quest/i/on

Who
is going to lead
now?

Biographies

Photo: Michael Spatola

Hadley Fitzgerald, M.A., M.F.T., has been a licensed psychotherapist almost as long as she's been an astrologer. She is the author of the Psychological Astrology section of *Under One Sky* by Rafael Nasser, ed. by Jodie Forrest. Once upon a time she had visions of becoming a Shakespearean scholar, but her daimon had other plans. She has published numerous articles and has been a free-lance writer for more than 25 years. She has a certificate of training in Ecopsychology from the Institute for Cultural Change and is also a Certified Tarotpy® Practitioner.

"In addition to our being part of a planetary ecosystem, I believe we each have a deep internal archetypal ecology to establish, maintain, and nourish. To me, the birthchart provides a multi-dimensional illustration of that ecology. It shows us the soul's best intentions for this incarnation, the ways we can resonate consciously with those intentions, and how we might thoughtfully deal with the challenges to our earthly progress as well as our spiritual evolution."

While traditional therapeutic methods are her foundation, Hadley often expands on those methods by using astrology's ancient archetypal symbols to help clients address the conundrums of individual and family dynamics on another level. When appropriate, she also brings in a wide variety of tarot and other images to explore the mythic dimensions of each life alongside the daily emotional issues, choices, and opportunities for expression that can aid the evolution of the soul as it travels through this lifetime. At the heart of her training and her work is this question: "What does your soul, your daimon, want of you, want *with* you?"

She has a love for what emerges in the process of writing, and an example of her poetry can be found on pages 171-172.

Email at FitzHere2@aol.com
Her website is:
www.HadleyFitzgerald.com or www.EternityRoad.com
Her office is in Sherman Oaks, California, and she can be reached at 818-783-3891

Photo: Rosine Sörbom

Judith Harte, Ph.D. M.F.T., is a licensed marriage and family therapist, and archetypal astrologer, with offices in Studio City and West Los Angeles, California. She has a burgeoning interest in clay sculpture, and spends much of her free time actively creating images of soul out of clay. Her sculpture "Offering" along with her short poetic piece, known as an *ekphrasis,* were written concurrently as the sculpture emerged and are presented on page 167.

"The most tragic of our life struggles may seem less tragic and more meaningful when viewed through the layered lens of the arts, the time-honored tales of myth and dreams, the poignant and/or uplifting tones of music, and yes, the exciting theater of one's astrological horoscope. I have a great love for the astrological language, which is the language of myth and story. Whether astrological, or psychological, I respect the coexistence and interplay of both these modes of perceiving psyche. And there are, in fact, many licensed psychotherapists worldwide who share my views."

Not only does her work embrace the mythic and depth dimensions of human experience, she also has a clinical practice with an emphasis upon crisis intervention, hospice, and coping with ordinary problems of daily living.

Her work has been shown in the "Mirrors of Your Mind" exhibitions sponsored by the Los Angeles County Psychological Association [LACPA], created especially for and by psychotherapists who are also artists. She is the author of a poetry collection entitled *Father Complex*, written while transiting Saturn was conjunct her Scorpio Sun.

Email at Jharte1@aol.com, @Judith Harte on Twitter.
Her website is www.ImagesOfSoul.com
She can be reached via voice mail at 310 281-7991

Bibliograpy

Boer, Charles. *Marsilio Ficino: The Book of Life*. A translation by Charles Boer. Irving, TX: Spring Publications, 1980.

Casey, Caroline W. *Making the Gods Work for You: The Astrological Language of the Psyche*. New York: Harmony Books, 1998.

Cooper, J.C. *An Illustrated Encyclopedia of Traditional Symbols*. London: Thames and Hudson, 1978.

Forrest, Steven. *Yesterday's Sky: Astrology and Reincarnation*. Borrego Springs, CA: Seven Paws Press, 2008.

Hillman, James. *Insearch: Psychology and Religion*. Dallas, TX: Spring Publications, 1967.

Hillman, James. *Re-Visioning Psychology*. New York: Harper & Row, 1975.

Hillman, James. *Facing the Gods*. Dallas, TX: Spring Publications, 1980.

Hillman, James. *The Thought of the Heart*. Eranos Lecture Series 2. Dallas, TX: Spring Publications, 1984.

Hillman, James. *The Soul's Code: In Search of Character and Calling*. New York: Random House, 1996.

Hillman, James. and Sonu Shamdasani. *Lament of the Dead: Psychology after Jung's Red Book.* New York: W.W. Norton & Co. 2013.

Idemon, Richard. *The Magic Thread: Astrological Chart Interpretation Using Depth Psychology.* York Beach, ME: Samuel Weiser, Inc., 1996.

Liddell & Scott. *An Intermediate Greek-English Lexicon,* 7th Edition. Oxford: Oxford University Press, 1997.

Lockhart, Russell. *Words as Eggs: Psyche in Language and Clinic.* Dallas, TX: Spring Publications, 1983.

Miller, David. *Masks of Creativity.* Public Lecture. Washington, D.C., 1988.

Moore, Thomas. *The Planets Within: Marsilio Ficino's Astrological Psychology.* London and Toronto: Associated University Presses, 1982.

Poncé, Charles. "Medusa: A New look at an Old Face." Public lecture C.G. Jung Institute. Los Angeles, CA, 1980.

Poncé, Charles. *Papers Toward a Radical Metaphysics.* Berkeley, CA: North Atlantic Books, 1983.

Rilke, Rainer Maria. *Letters to a Young Poet.* New York: W.W. Norton, 1934.

Rodale, J.I. *The Synonym Finder.* Emmaus, PA: Rodale Press, 1978.

Schwartz-Salant, Nathan. *Narcissism and Character Transformation: The Psychology of Narcissistic Character Disorders.* Canada: Inner City Books, 1982.

Tarnas, Richard. *Cosmos and Psyche: Intimations of a New World View*, New York: Viking-Penguin Group, 2006.

Watkins, Mary. *Waking Dreams.* New York: Gordon & Breach, 1976.

Watkins, Mary. "Six Approaches to the image in art therapy." Spring: An Annual of Archetypal Psychology and Jungian Thought. Zurich: Spring Publications, 1981.